ADVANCE PRAISE FOR
CHEAT ON YOUR HUSBAN

"The overall message of this bool up!
Go an
ins eful
str dowski Jr.,
nships.com

"W a useful
col age—and
wh ignant is
the her own
ma elf."

w mediator

"A to dating
tha aches you
ho\ e person,
not and you'll
be

g author of
The Secret

"A say that
A en who
re elf—and
ne re."

d *Boy Vey!*

"\ sh points
ou or us, are
of ou out of
your old, broken dating patterns, nothing else will."

—Evan Marc Katz, dating coach and coauthor of *Why You're Still Single*

CHEAT ON YOUR HUSBAND

(with Your Husband)

HOW TO DATE YOUR SPOUSE

ANDREA SYRTASH

© 2011 by Andrea Syrtash

Rodale books may be purchased for business or promotional use or for special sales. For information, please write to: Special Markets Department, Rodale Inc., 733 Third Avenue, New York, NY 10017.

Printed in the United States of America
Rodale Inc. makes every effort to use acid-free ⊗, recycled paper ⊚.

Book design by Christina Guagler

Library of Congress Cataloging-in-Publication Data
Syrtash, Andrea.
    Cheat on your husband (with your husband): how to date your spouse/ Andrea Syrtash.
        p.   cm.
    Includes index.
    ISBN 978–1–60961–109–5 paperback
    1. Marriage.   2. Wives—Conduct of life.   3. Wives—Sexual behavior.
4. Man-woman relationships.   I. Title.
HQ734.S988   2011
646.7'8—dc23

Distributed to the trade by Macmillan
2   4   6   8   10   9   7   5   3   1   paperback

We inspire and enable people to improve their lives and the world around them.
www.rodalebooks.com

This book is dedicated to jugglers—those of you who manage to juggle all of your many respon- sibilities to your family, career, community, and, hopefully, to your own personal expression.

A successful marriage requires falling in love many times,
always with the same person.

—MIGNON MCLAUGHLIN

CONTENTS

PROLOGUE: WE'RE ALL TEENAGERS
WHEN WE FALL IN LOVE..xi

Part One: Modern Marriage

Chapter One: This Is Your Brain on Love
(It's All about Chemistry. Literally.) 3

Chapter Two: This Is Not Your Mother's Marriage............ 18

Chapter Three. Turn ME On................................38

Chapter Four: Words, Words, Words................................60

Chapter Five: Take a Time Out: Cheat On Your Kids..........78

Part Two: Stop Complaining and Start Creating

Chapter Six: Cheating On Your Husband
(with Someone Who's Not Your Husband) 101

Chapter Seven: Cheat On Your Husband
(with Your Husband)....................................117

Chapter Eight: Let's Talk about Sex 132

Chapter Nine: Sweat the Small Stuff................................152

Chapter Ten: Be the Partner You Want to Have................169

CONCLUSION: WHAT'S NEXT?....................................189

ACKNOWLEDGMENTS... 203

ABOUT THE AUTHOR 207

PROLOGUE

We're All Teenagers When We Fall in Love

Do you remember the way your husband looked at you when you first started dating him? Chances are you looked at yourself differently then, too. Whether you were 13 or 30 at the time, odds are you felt like a teenager.

I'm certain that I reverted to a giddy 15-year-old girl when I first fell for my husband, Michael. I was 30 at the time. Our first kiss felt like . . . my first kiss. I had major butterflies, displayed an endearing (in my mind, at least) amount of awkwardness, and felt a little mischievous during our first embrace—like we might get caught. Time stood still. And other clichés applied. All the love songs on the radio spoke to me; I couldn't imagine ever looking at or wanting to be with another man. I wore underwear that actually matched my bra.

And today? While I vividly remember feeling like a teenager, now there are times when I feel like an old nagging woman reminding Michael, for the zillionth time, to pick up his socks. (What is it about men leaving a trail of socks around the home? I've decided that it must date back to the trails that men had to leave in the forest to find their way back to their huts.) I'm guessing that marriage feels different from dating not only for me, but for many of you as well.

LIFE BEFORE MARRIAGE

Chances are you had settled into a full and fulfilling life before you got married—one that included a group of great friends, vacations and weekend getaways, nights out on the town, and perhaps a demanding job you secretly enjoyed devoting too many hours to. In those days, you didn't have to check in with anyone if you were going to stay late, head to the gym after work, or eat dinner early. You enjoyed living on your own or with a roommate or two, and you were content indulging in your own schedule. This doesn't mean you did not imagine—or desire—a loving partner to share your life with, but you didn't *need* that "special someone" to feel as though your life was meaningful.

When you started dating your (now) husband, you may have been struck with the feeling that things could be even more fun and interesting with him around. Life was good, but with this guy, it could be even better. You had dated enough duds to know that this man was different. You were impressed with him, and with yourself around him. You were charming and witty, patient and kind. (I recently read an e-mail that I sent to Michael during our first few months of dating, and I wanted to hang out with the girl I was then!) Your husband brought out the best in you, and being with him became one of your favorite pastimes. The thought of many more hours and years in his presence delighted you. Otherwise, why would you have given up your single status?

Now that you've settled down and have more responsibilities, you may no longer see yourself as the self-assured woman who goes after what she wants, or as the patient and playful woman who is fun to be around. You may marvel that the man you now live with is the same one who pursued you, who once planned creative dates and left sweet, funny, or seductive messages on your voice mail.

The reality is that life doesn't always make it easy to prioritize the connection you have with your husband in the same way you once did, and your relationship often falls to the bottom of your long to-do list.

Every day, single women approach me for advice about how to keep the men they're dating intrigued and interested and how to stay interesting themselves. I recently realized how few of us in long-term relationships ask ourselves these questions, even though they should still be relevant to our relationships. In fact, I believe these questions are even more relevant for those in long-term partnerships.

Too many women wake up in their marriages and wonder, "Is this really it?" They wonder if they're still the women they once were, or the women they want to be now. They can't help but question if they are living the life they intended to have. And as scientists have come to understand, there is a very real biological difference between how it feels to fall in love and how it feels to *be* in love. This is actually good news—it's totally normal to no longer daydream about your spouse or have hot fantasies about him when you're apart. It's completely common to trade in the G-strings for Spanx (right?). But just because you settle down doesn't mean you have to settle for a life you don't love.

DATING MY HUSBAND

When I began thinking about the topic for this book, I was inspired by the desire to keep my own marriage fresh and dynamic. The night before my wedding ceremony in 2006, I gave myself a pep talk that included an intimate promise. "I will hold on to who I am and embrace who I can be. And I will always try to have fun."

The last part of my quiet secular prayer slipped out unexpectedly. In fact, it surprised me. I was entering a serious spiritual

xiv   PROLOGUE

partnership governed by the law and I was thinking about *fun?*
I was committing to a union with the man I loved and I was
making a promise to *myself?*

For better or for worse, it was a choice I made and one that
I am thankful for. Without fun, marriage is all work. Without
work, it also doesn't work. Whoever came up with the idea of
happily ever after should have put in a disclaimer: Marriage—
and the commitment that goes along with it—*is a choice you
have to make every day.* It's up to you to create your own
happy ending.

Throughout the book, I will refer to the experiences of
women in various stages of marriage—from the first year to the
50-year mark—to help illustrate my main premise: that marriage can be more fun, fulfilling, and exceptional than you
might think. I will share the latest research on marriage and
brain activity during love and reveal the best strategies for communication and connection. As your coach, I will challenge you
to challenge yourself by putting verbs in your sentences. (In other
words, there will be homework! But trust me, it won't be of the
nightmare-inducing variety.)

None of the women you will meet in the pages that follow
have taken a passive role in their relationships, even when things
got tough (especially when things got tough). Each understands
that she is not a passenger in her marriage or her life, and that
a healthy partnership requires two drivers who may contribute
different elements but who both ensure that the relationship
moves forward. These women know that they can't be good
wives, good mothers, or happy people if they don't take care of
their own needs. They realize that they can't be engaged in their
marriages if they are not engaged in their own lives outside their
marriage. They are aware that the dynamic of a relationship is
affected by how they act and react.

You will also meet women who feel frustrated by the challenges of balancing their roles as women, wives, and mothers. These women, who can't remember the last time they monotasked, struggle daily to find the fun and joy in their marriages. They've generously shared their process of discovery in the hopes that it may spark some ideas and action that will benefit all of us.

While it's true that almost half of marriages end in divorce today, it is also true that married couples live longer than singles, and married women and men report being happiest. When you committed to your partner, what did you want? How close are you to your vision of marriage?

Sometimes you don't realize how much you miss your romantic connection with your spouse until days, weeks, months, and years have passed. Don't wait for alarm bells to go off to jolt you into action. Why wait to fix your relationship until it's in crisis? The time is always now. It is never too late to reinvent (or recapture) yourself and your relationship. If you don't realign with your priorities, nobody else will.

It's time to stop complaining—and to start creating!

PART ONE

MODERN MARRIAGE

You might think that a book with a name like *Cheat On Your Husband* would be dedicated to the topics of infidelity, sex, and play. But I've never been one to rush into sex without getting to know someone. We women need more than sex to fall deeply in love. We may not initially notice a man or think of him as our type, but after sharing a dynamic conversation or great experience together, we may become attracted to him. I know that the way a man stimulates my mind and makes me laugh increases my desire to know what he would be like between the sheets and in a relationship. There is a direct correlation among my brain, my body, and wanting to take action.

For this reason, I want to hold off on the bedroom talk before you get to know me (and you) a little better. Think of these first few chapters as mental foreplay. In Part One, we'll cover everything from how your brain operates in love to why your mother's marriage advice may not be applicable to you. We'll explore how to reframe the dynamic of your relationship so you are communicating effectively, and we will look at the best ways to create balance in your overbooked life so that your marriage is still an exciting priority. We will also explore the impact of being a mom on your marriage and offer creative solutions for how to deal with parenting responsibilities without ignoring your most important relationship of all.

This book is not just about reconnecting with your husband; it's also, and perhaps more important, about reconnecting with *yourself.* What do you miss about who you were when you met your spouse? What vision do you hold for your future? After all, you can't be passionate about your marriage if you're not passionate about your own life.

But before you can change the way you act, you need to change the way you think. So let's start with the basis of all thought: your brain.

CHAPTER ONE

This Is Your Brain on Love

(It's All about Chemistry. Literally.)

There's an old joke that after years of marriage, a man complains, "She changed!" and a woman complains, "He didn't change!" Just as change is a part of life, it's also a part of marriage—a very healthy and normal part of it.

When you first met your spouse, chances are you were in a different job, city, or situation than you are in today. You likely approached your relationship differently because 1) you were different, 2) he was different, and 3) times were different.

But have you considered that your relationship feels different because your *brain chemistry* is different?

In 2002, biological anthropologist Dr. Helen Fisher joined Dr. Lucy Brown, a professor of neurology and neuroscience, and Dr. Art Aron, a professor of psychology, to conduct an experiment on the science of love. In the study, Dr. Fisher and her colleagues worked with 17 students who reported being madly in love. These students, all of whom admitted that they thought about their love most hours of the waking day (upwards of 80 percent of the time!), were brought into a lab where their brains were scanned while they completed a series of exercises.

Each set of exercises lasted for 12 minutes. First, Dr. Fisher showed each subject a photo of his or her object of affection for 30 seconds. Next, the subject would be asked to count backward (to clear the brain of the feelings of romantic love and passion). Finally, the subject would stare at a neutral photograph for 30 seconds, perhaps of someone he or she vaguely knew, before being asked to count again. The cycle was repeated half a dozen times, ensuring that Dr. Fisher and her team were able to accurately capture the person's brain activity.

What this team of experts discovered has revolutionized the way we think about love. The study showed that romantic love is not simply an emotion, as many of us would believe; rather, it is a biological and chemical response that starts in the brain.

One region that showed tremendous activity when subjects gazed at photos of their beloved was the *caudate nucleus*, a relatively small area in the center of the brain that is one of the oldest, most primitive parts of the human brain. Linked to cravings and to the brain's "reward system," the caudate becomes activated by stimuli we find highly desirable—like money or chocolate . . . or love. Dr. Fisher's experiment demonstrated that romantic love cues our reward system and affects us on the most primal level.

People often talk about how love lives in the heart and not in the head, but in reality, it is the brain that convinces us that the love we desire will make everything else in life feel perfect. Dr. Fisher argues that the drive toward love can be more powerful than the drive toward hunger. As it turns out, we are wired to pursue romantic love, as our brains perceive it as one of the greatest rewards life has to offer.

I often joke that during the first 3 months of dating, everyone is lying, because we tend to present the best versions of ourselves to potential mates. But there is some truth in this statement. At the start of courtship, when you are attracted and interested in someone, there is a tendency to mirror one another and to find uncanny similarities. Most of this "we are exactly alike!" response happens on a subconscious level (therefore, you may have actually believed you really did love hockey when you told your future spouse he or she should invest in season tickets). We are so eager to mate with the objects of our affection (especially when the caudate is activated) that our brains will do anything to keep us connected.

People in the early stages of romantic love demonstrate the obsessive thinking patterns that are common in people who have obsessive compulsive disorder (OCD). And the brain chemistry of addiction is also often displayed in the brains of people falling in love. Dr. Fisher's initial hypothesis, that increased levels of the neurotransmitters dopamine and norepinephrine would be associated with feelings of romantic love, proved to be correct. Dopamine is a brain chemical linked to feelings of elation and joy. Norepinephrine produces an adrenaline-like rush usually set off by stress, but in the case of romantic love, the hormone manifests as giddy excitement that makes someone's palms sweat or heart race when she is around the object of her affection. Both neurochemicals contribute to increased focus and a surge in energy, which is why new love feels so intoxicating. According to Dr. John Marsden of the British National Addiction Center, who has also studied the brain in love, the effects of this love cocktail make us immensely euphoric and can be as powerful as a drug.

When we are in the early romantic love stage, we operate in a suspended reality in which adequate sleep and food seem less necessary (as if love is all the nourishment we need) and in which our judgment is clouded. The part of our brain responsible for experiencing fear (or being cautious), the amygdala, is less active when we are falling in love.

In other words, brain chemicals like dopamine that are generated when we are falling for someone are dope—fun and potentially dangerous. And, like the effect of drugs, the high we experience is fleeting. We cannot sustain the heady rush of romantic love once the onslaught of intoxicating chemicals subsides and our brains settle into a more stable, predictable state. With the right marriage ingredients, however, the pleasure center of the brain can still show tremendous activity even after decades with the same person. More on that later.

Let's return to you, when you first started dating your spouse-to-be, and when your caudate nucleus was shining brightly.

EVERYTHING LOOKS BETTER WHEN YOU'RE FALLING IN LOVE (INCLUDING YOU)

Think back to the time you first met your husband. What did your life look like then? What kind of job did you have? Where did you live? What were your interests? How did you look? And when you began a relationship with him, how did you feel? Nervous? Excited? Did you experience happy sleepless nights and increased focus, like the love-struck people in Dr. Fisher's experiment? Or did you grow attracted to your partner over time and through shared experiences with him?

When I first started dating Michael, I was a superhuman who required only 4 hours of sleep a night and very little (except for time with him) to be happy. During the first few months of our relationship, food tasted better, I had more patience, and the world looked positively rosy. I remember pointing out a tree to my friend and saying, "Isn't that oak fantastic?!" despite the fact that I'd walked by that same tree for years. I had never quite noticed it before.

When I was in the first phase of love, I was like one of those cartoon characters skipping through the neighborhood followed by animated birds and butterflies. I was on the trippy dopamine ride and prepared to do anything to make the relationship work. Michael was on the ride, too. We stayed up for hours talking, and he never appeared to be tired. Now that I've lived with him for a few years, I know that without adequate rest he's moody; but in those days, he displayed one mood—and it was happy.

My friend Raquel, who has been married for 6 years and is the mother of a toddler, admitted that she had a number of clichéd moments when she first started dating her husband, Matt: "When I met Matt, he was so darn cute. I thought his smile was amazing—bright and shiny. On our first date, I came downstairs and it was like time stood still. We both looked at each other and it seemed that nothing was said for ages. It hit me—bam! There was chemistry."

And now? I asked Raquel if Matt still takes her breath away. Her voice dropped a couple of octaves. "He is cute and I'm used to it, I guess. It's just . . . Matt. I would be excited to feel desire again . . . but I'm tired." She paused and reflected, "I guess I don't see him with sparkles anymore. Now things feel different. I *wanted* him before and now I *need* him. He's a part of my life—like family."

Are we supposed to see our spouses like *family?* Raquel admitted that she didn't know the answer to that question. She finds it confusing, and even a little disconcerting, to feel a different kind of love than the kind she used to feel for her partner. She doesn't know how she *should* feel, and how could she? Nobody has been in her marriage before, and she has no frame of reference.

"I don't know what I expected marriage to be like," Raquel acknowledged, "so I don't know if my experience is normal."

I've always found the statement "I don't know how I should feel" strange. *Should* and *feel* don't go together. How do you feel?

GREAT EXPECTATIONS

I often say that everything in life is about managing expectations.

I recently made a book appearance in a small town in the Northeast and stayed at a hotel in the town's center. Days before arriving, I read online reviews about the "creepy" front-desk man and the "decrepit" rooms at the hotel. But by then, everything else in the area was booked. So I prepared myself for a dismal stay. I even brought my own pillow and towel.

Upon checking in, I noticed that the "creepy" front-desk guy was eccentric and sweet. It was true that the hotel had not been renovated in years, but I found the place had a real 19th-century charm that I enjoyed. It was located on a beautiful property in a fantastic part of town. My room was clean, simple, and comfortable. The hotel didn't provide shampoo, but I knew that from the reviews, so I had packed a trial size of Pert Plus. No big deal.

I, too, might have shared a similar negative write-up about the accommodations on the travel Web site if I had arrived at the quaint hotel expecting a flat-screen television and 1,000-thread-count Egyptian cotton sheets. Instead, I was pleasantly surprised that nothing crawled in the room and that I found a good place for a good price. I posted a nice online review and mentioned I would return since I felt at home instantly.

What happens when you don't know what to expect? If only there were Internet reviews when it came to your marriage.

Raquel wondered, "Am I supposed to feel how I used to feel about my husband? If so, is this marriage in trouble? When you start questioning your feelings all the time, you make meaning out of it and put pressure on yourself. I have a friend who doesn't know if she's in love with her husband anymore, though she cares for him deeply. Does that mean her marriage isn't good?"

While I can't tell you how you *should* feel after years in a relationship with the same person, more information about the next phase of love, the attachment phase, might help put things into perspective. According to Dr. Fisher's research, falling in love and being in love are biologically different experiences.

Couples who are in a romantic relationship enter the attachment stage somewhere between 12 months and 3 years of being together. During this love phase, which is characterized by feelings of comfort and connection with your partner, the chemicals oxytocin and vasopressin are released in your brain.

Oxytocin is the same hormone that is released when a woman has an orgasm, gives birth, or is breastfeeding her baby. It stimulates our maternal instincts. It has even been referred to as "the cuddle hormone," as it elicits soothing and comforting feelings.

The attachment stage feels very different from the lusty first phase of dating. It may be dangerous to raise children when you are addicted to romantic love and not thinking clearly, so nature has made this next love phase more calm and stable. In a sense, you and your partner return to normal programming. Your mind is not consumed by thoughts of your lover, and you may not have the same desire to make out or to wear makeup. Once your brain has removed its rosy glasses, you realize your boyfriend has morning breath and isn't always charming. Not to worry. The attachment phase is a good thing. You begin to realize that this is the person you want to call first when you get good news or bad. You rely on each other and your bond is strong. Attachment helps us live longer, healthier, and happier lives, which is why the US Department of Health and Human Services invested $1.2 billion between 2005 and 2010 promoting programs that encourage getting and staying married. In the attachment stage, you see your partner differently, and perhaps you see yourself differently as well.

THINK ABOUT IT

Your perspective influences you every day. Studies show that our brain chemistry is affected by the way we process life's events. The neural network in your brain is constantly learning, adapting, and changing.

The funny thing about perspective is that once you settle on a particular viewpoint, you start seeing everything through that lens. Have you ever bought a new car and then noticed that suddenly every car on the road seems to be the same as yours? In a way, you lose your peripheral vision when you get stuck on a particular point of view.

Every day in your relationship, you choose a perspective about your husband and your life and you collect evidence to support it. If your perspective is "He doesn't ever contribute," you will be extra-annoyed when you walk by him lounging in front of the television, and you may not even notice when he takes out the trash. If your perspective is "My husband is really thoughtful," you're more likely to recognize the small gestures he makes to ensure you are happy. And if your perspective of marriage is "all work and no play," you may not see the joy, passion, and fulfillment that a committed partnership can bring. You may not even give yourself the chance to be fulfilled in your marriage.

What's one of the negative perspectives you have about your husband? Maybe you think, "He doesn't do enough around the home." Is there a more positive perspective you can focus on? You might choose to focus on a perspective like "He works hard to provide for our family."

WHAT DOES YOUR MARRIAGE LOOK LIKE?

Many people characterize dating as being full of potential and possibilities, since it's a time when everything is exciting and unknown. Marriage, on the other hand, is typically characterized by different Ps—partnership and perseverance (and, usually, problems).

Couples often share stories of how they met, when they first fell in love, or where they got engaged. How many times have you heard a couple recount the tales of their first year of marriage or parenthood? It's as if the story of our relationship ends once we've walked down the aisle.

But the heart of our love story—and the most interesting and dynamic chapters in our relationship—happen after the dopamine has dissipated and we become attached to our partners. Falling in love and getting married are simple, but staying married—happily married—is a challenge.

We forget that as much as marriage relies on partnership and perseverance for sustenance, it thrives on potential and possibilities. Just because you know all of your partner's corny jokes, favorite stories, and cute (and let's face it, sometimes irritating) idiosyncrasies, that doesn't mean you've learned everything about him or can predict the outcome of your lives together. You and your spouse are meant to grow individually and as a couple over time. Your love story doesn't end at "I do"—it is always evolving.

When you're several years into your relationship, the love goggles may come off, but they're replaced by new lenses that reveal another, fuller picture of your relationship. Dori, who has been married to her husband, Seth, for 5 years and is the mother of a toddler, admitted, "Dating was full of angst and unknowns. The greatest part of marriage is knowing we're in it. There's much less pressure. As soon as you're married, after the wedding, you can relax. You got there, you've done it. This is it— you don't have to do anything anymore."

Dori and her husband both agree that dating was difficult, and they love the security of knowing that they're "in it" together. Through their lens, marriage is stable and solid. Neither of them craves the drama and unpredictability that dating brought into their lives. They are just starting to realize, though, that comfort can breed complacency. The idea of date nights, with time away from their little boy, has recently come up as something they want to explore, since they haven't connected with each other in the way they used to.

Seth admitted, "There's been so much transition over the last couple years—new home, new baby, new career—that the times my wife and I have gone out, just the two of us, are few and far between. For me, personally, it's important to have that. I want to go out and do even simple things alone with Dori. We recently went out for ice cream and a movie and had a great, great time. I didn't realize how much I missed that connection. To keep our sanity and have fun—we need that in our marriage."

I interviewed a 33-year-old woman who said she feels less relaxed as a mother and wife than she was as a single woman in Manhattan. Through her lens, she sees the loss of freedom that marriage and motherhood brought into her life. "When I was single, I could pick up and go to a concert, the movies, or book a last-minute vacation with girlfriends," she said. "I miss the ease and independence of singlehood."

I read this woman's statement to a client of mine, who at 39 years old has been single for the past 4 years since moving out of her boyfriend's apartment. My client sighed, "Tell her we can trade lives. I'd love to have other people—a great husband and children—to depend on me. Sometimes I wonder if anybody would notice if I didn't go home for days. It can get very lonely. It would be nice to have someone else in my court."

When we're single, we crave the stability of a guaranteed date on Saturday night and lazy Sunday mornings spent with someone special. I've often heard singles describe the pursuit of finding a mate as exhausting. Then, when we're married, we crave the excitement and independence of our premarriage lives—from fun nights out with our girlfriends to Sundays spent doing our own thing in solitude.

Do we have to choose only one side—being free and enjoying our lives, or being stable and having security? What about the couples out there (and we all know a few) who seem to have a solid foundation but who also have fun together? The truth is, feeling secure, sexy, and self-expressed are not mutually exclusive qualities in a marriage.

The happy couples we know embrace all four Ps (potential, possibilities, perseverance, and partnership). They are committed to themselves and their partnerships and to creating new experiences. They realize that they have to take an active role in their lives and their relationships to find a happy balance.

Take Matt and Sari, who have been together for 11 years and who both have demanding jobs in addition to family duties. Fitting in regular weekend "day sex" (while the kids are napping) and leaving little sweet notes keep both partners on their toes. Matt and Sari have structured their marriage to have fun as much as they've committed to keeping their marriage grounded. They communicate often, encourage the other to develop his or her passions on a regular basis, and carve out time away from their two kids for dating each other. Recently, they went out to a jazz club so they could hear good music and explore a new neighborhood.

Matt said, "We need a date night at least once a month—it's a priority in our relationship. I think it's important to create new and interesting memories with Sari, but even when we just go to the movies, we hold hands and feel like teens again. It's refreshing to get away from household duties and connect the way we used to. We take long walks together, since that's something we used to love to do when we were dating. We promise each other that we won't spend our entire date talking about our kids!"

Sari added that it's unrealistic to think you're always going to want to be romantic with your spouse or going to feel like putting in the extra effort, so you have to put a structure in place to make sure adults-only time is a priority. In a way, she's reminding married couples not to wait for inspiration to strike since, in reality, you may be too tired to even realize what you're missing.

A month before her wedding day, Sari's mother told her to expect that there will be times she won't look at her husband the way she used to. There will be times she may *love* him but not *like* him. It makes Sari worry less that she needs to feel attracted and excited about her husband all the time. She knows marriage is not a fairy tale and has managed her expectations without becoming passive in her relationship. She agrees with her husband that a monthly outing together helps nourish their connection and admits that even when she doesn't initially feel like planning a night out, she is always glad they did it.

Duncan and Martine, who have been together for more than a decade and married for 5 of those years, make sure to create time every week to be together. When Duncan isn't on the road touring as a musician, he and Martine both work at home. Most days, they break for lunch together and power off their computers at a particular hour at night so they can make dinner and share quality time. They've had to create a structure to connect as husband and wife, they told me, or they could easily get caught up in living as roommates and co-workers.

Duncan said, "A few times a week, we'll make dinner, open a nice bottle of wine, and talk a lot. I really love spending this time with my wife, and it's a highlight of our week. We both appreciate it."

Martine mentioned that she and Duncan communicate with each other when one or both of them feel that too much time has passed without connecting for longer than a few minutes. In those instances, they'll take out their calendars. "We'll say, 'I miss hanging out with you—let's pick a date!'" Martine said. They always plan to spend time together, even when schedules are busy.

Couples like these, who are committed to spending time together and keeping romance at the forefront of their marriages, may not realize that they are actually tricking their brains into thinking their love is new. Doing novel things with each other, sharing interesting experiences, and creating an element of surprise together increase the levels of dopamine in their brains— therefore registering their connections as being in the early romantic stage. Consistently and consciously creating new memories together helps these couples to view marriage as fun and fulfilling.

I also talked to women who felt drained by the demands of marriage and have trouble seeing their relationships as anything other than work. Once your thought patterns lean this way, your brain settles on that perspective, making it difficult to seek out the romance and passion you're missing with your partner. It's like what happens when you're in a job you don't like. I know that when I've had a job with few rewards and little potential for growth, I certainly haven't looked forward to reporting to work. In those instances, I've gone through the motions, and my work suffered as a result.

When you view your marriage as all work, it's hard to see how anything could change for the better. You may look in the rearview mirror, missing what you used to have or who you used to be or how you once looked.

Lori, a mother of two teenagers, explained, "It's very enticing to think about starting again with someone new, who I don't share so much baggage with and who has the energy and interest to pursue me. I used to feel sexy with my husband. I want that feeling again."

When I asked Lori what *she* contributes to creating a sexy space in her marriage, and what she does to connect in new and different ways with her spouse, she went back to complaining about her husband's lack of romance. It's as if she doesn't see herself in the picture of her marriage.

Women like Lori, who fantasize about escaping their "boring" situations, forget that love unfolds in cycles. New love will always feel vibrant and passionate. Eventually, after the high with someone new wears off, a woman will once again return to boredom if she continues to be a passive participant in her relationship. It's up to both parties to reinvent and reinforce the romance and connection that they are missing. Keeping the proverbial spark alive requires putting out fires where they don't need to spread and igniting fires in other areas. That's the work of relationships, and it's the choice you have to make each day of your marriage.

WHAT PICTURE OF MARRIAGE DO YOU WANT TO SEE?

There is a place between being addicted to love and resigning yourself to a lifetime of "work."

I am not asking you to emulate who you were when you first met your husband. For one thing, that would be boring—you've been there before! It's also not very practical. Back then, you likely had different ideas and priorities and a different way of being in the world. As we know, your brain was even different when you first met your spouse, even if that was only a couple of years ago.

As a relationship coach and journalist, I have worked with couples who struggle to maintain their connection because they admit that the demands of their busy lives make romance and fun with their spouses low priorities. They are operating on autopilot, pressing the snooze button every day instead of waking up to the possibilities of their marriage. Their excuses—such as being overtired, overworked, and overextended—are all valid. These days, we have more things competing for our attention than ever before. It's not easy to give your spouse and your marriage attention when you barely have time to get through the day, but it is possible and, I would add, necessary.

It starts with shifting your perspective from *saving* your marriage to *creating* the marriage you want. You don't need to be in repair mode to take action and to start committing to thinking and doing things differently. A healthy marriage requires regular maintenance, occasional checkups, and consistent growth. And a few failures along the way with expectations in check. You won't learn what you need without discovering what doesn't work. It's essential to stay open to all the possibilities, even the messy ones, that a committed partnership will bring.

You've grown and changed since you met your spouse, and because of that you have more to offer now. In fact, it's a great thing that your brain chemistry has changed and rebalanced since dating your husband. Let's face it, none of us would be productive members of society if we experienced such obsessive thoughts all day! We wouldn't contribute much to the world. We would become terribly boring.

The process of cheating on your husband with your husband is about cheating some of the rules you've heard about what it means to be a "good wife" or a "perfect mother." It's about creating a new picture of partnership that excites you and inspires you. It is also about maximizing the last love stage with your spouse, the one that will carry your relationship and move it into the future. After all, this phase with your partner is where the real magic of your own growth and the possibilities of your relationship unfold. It is where the high you experience is even higher—because it's not based on a sugary recipe that will eventually make you crash, but on natural ingredients that will sustain you over time and provide the best soul nourishment. When you learn to savor this stage, it can be the most delicious one of all.

CHAPTER TWO

This Is Not Your Mother's Marriage

Many years ago, I was watching a TV talk show on which an elderly woman shared her secret to her 60-plus-year marriage. The host asked how she and her husband made their marriage work after many decades together. She answered simply, "My husband and I never fell out of love at the same time."

When marriage was invented (thousands of years ago), few people were toasting their 80th birthdays or celebrating their 60th wedding anniversaries. Life spans were shorter and, therefore, so were marriages. Now, with medical breakthroughs and developments in the field of biotech that are increasingly extending our life spans (some researchers speculate that in the not-too-distant future, many of us will live well into our hundreds), the idea of making a marriage last for eternity may feel like a life sentence.

Throughout most of history, marriage was regarded as a practical union that ensured a family's bloodline and protected its financial and social status. Families often arranged the pairing of their children, something they still do in many cultures around the world today. Matrimony was essentially a business transaction, and love was not a necessary ingredient. Some married couples grew to love each other immensely, some did not. It almost didn't matter.

Over the past century, the average age at which American women marry has increased by 4.4 years (from 21.6 in 1910 to 26 in 2010). Even though less than half a decade may not seem like a big jump, it is significant. Women today are deferring marriage until they've gone to school, started careers, and had significant life experiences. According to sociologist Andrew J. Cherlin, "Marriage used to be the first step into adulthood. Now it is often the last."

Back in the Old Country (Canada, where I grew up), my aunts Dorothy and Sally married their husbands at the age of 18, soon after they graduated from high school. My mother, on the other hand, settled down later—she waited to finish university before she walked down the aisle with my dad at age 22.

At 22, I was moving into my own place for the first time and learning the basics of adulthood, like how to boil an egg and change a lightbulb. I was happily independent in my crammed studio apartment in New Jersey, with the dream of one day moving to New York City (and living in another, more expensive, crammed studio apartment) to launch my life and my career. I was also planning a whirlwind European adventure that I felt was my hard-earned right before entering the "real world." I needed to grow up and *find myself.* Marriage was the last thing on my mind.

By the time I turned 30, I had lived in six different cities, seen many countries, enjoyed a number of relationships, completed two academic degrees, earned a life-coaching certificate, and was celebrating the publication of my first book. I felt proud of the life I'd created and had a strong sense of who I was.

On my 30th birthday, my father reminded me that when my mother was 30, she was already a mother to me and my sister, Veronica. He mentioned that at my age, my mother had a steady career as a teacher, enjoyed a great lifestyle, and lived in a nice home that they had purchased with the money they had both earned from working hard. (I get it, Dad.)

I spoke with a bright and attractive 29-year-old woman recently who admitted that she is in no rush to get married until she has seen some of the world and paid off some of her student debt. Like many in her generation, she is more interested in settling into her life before she settles down.

Unlike me and many of the women I know, my grandmothers didn't expect to explore the world before getting married, and they didn't have student loans to pay off. They moved straight from their parents' homes to their new homes with their husbands. The idea of "finding themselves" was never part of their lexicon, even though they were both strong women.

Our generation strives for self-expression (some may argue that we demand it) in many areas of our lives, including in our romantic relationships and our careers. We consider that keeping our values and interests aligned is necessary for a happy life. Some may call this attitude spoiled or entitled. I think it is smart and enlightened.

I know that figuring out my career path was important to me, something I needed to achieve before I could imagine building a life with another person. I didn't need to have all the answers to my life figured out (I don't think we ever do), but I wanted to have a solid idea of who I was before adding another person to the mix.

In my first year of marriage, I remember telling my father that Michael wanted to be in a job that he was passionate about, to which my dad replied, "It's a job! Who says you're meant to like it?"

In our culture, we are incredibly fortunate to have great freedoms and opportunities. We seem to have an endless and sometimes overwhelming array of options, which leads many people to come down with a paralyzing case of WIMO (What If I Miss

Out?) syndrome. But it also means we don't feel as pressured to take one direct path toward adulthood as many of our parents and grandparents did. That path doesn't necessarily have to consist of school, marriage, house, two cars, job (for life), and babies (ideally 2.5). We often mix up the order and add and subtract many of these steps. For women today, getting married is a choice, and it is not one that we take lightly. We don't *need* a spouse to fulfill us. We can pay our own bills and have a child without having a partner. Nor do men need marriage today in the same way they once did. Bachelorhood has become a socially acceptable lifestyle, and most single men don't need to rely on a woman to tend their homes or cook their meals.

We are in the midst of an empowering singles movement supported by popular culture that depicts the upside of the single lifestyle (as evidenced by wildly successful syndicated television shows like *Sex and the City, Friends,* and *Two and a Half Men*).

Women in America are taking longer to settle down than ever before, according to recent census reports. A few years ago, the *New York Times* covered this trend in the article "51% of Women Are Now Living Without Spouse," which noted, "In 2005, married couples became a minority of all American households for the first time." The piece quoted single women between the ages of 24 and 59 who were asked why they were single. Some of the reasons they cited for delaying (or avoiding) marriage included the facts that they were "comfortable" in their lives and that they had seen too many friends' marriages end badly so were in no rush to walk down the aisle themselves. A 45-year-old woman stated, "I have not sworn off marriage, but if I do wed, it will be to have a companion with whom I can travel and play parlor games in my old age."

This trend isn't limited to American culture. In Japan, for instance, there are more single women between the ages of 20 and 40 than there are in the United States. According to a Japanese

34-year-old woman in New York whom I spoke with, "In some ways, marriage in Japan is still traditional. I'm happy with my life and would rather be single than unhappy. If I meet a nice man who I really like, that will be nice. If I don't, that's okay, too." She simply has no interest in taking on the traditional role of wife if it means giving up on her own needs.

Her perspective is especially shocking considering that just a few years ago, unmarried women in Japan over the age of 25 were often referred to as *kurisumasu keiki,* or Christmas cake; the connotation being that cake bought after the 25th would be old and undesirable. The festival of Hinamatsuri, or Girls' Day, is still celebrated in Japan, in which it is customary for families to perform certain rituals so that their daughters will grow up with the fortune to find good husbands. (Preparing a soup containing clams is one aspect of this celebration, as it is believed that the clamshells symbolize a peaceful union between a man and a woman.) "Good wife, wise mother" is still a popular cultural phrase, but the woman I interviewed, and many of her peers back in Japan, simply has no interest in taking on the traditional role of wife if it means giving up on her own needs.

I spoke with an American woman named Carol, who recently celebrated her 80th birthday and who has been widowed twice. She admires women today who take time to get to know themselves and who do not rush into marriage. She said, "In my era, there were a bunch of Stepford wives. Women's interests were almost irrelevant. I believe every woman should know who she is inside and outside of her marriage."

ROLE-PLAYING

My friend's parents, David and Dolores, who have been married for 37 years, commented on how clear-cut roles used to be within a marriage. In a way, they said, marriage seemed simpler in past generations because the roles of husband and wife—and expectations that came along with them—were clearly defined.

"Both David's father and mine were the breadwinners, and our mothers were the homemakers," Dolores remarked. "Our fathers expected a home-cooked meal, the kids to be taken care of, and their laundry to be done. Our mothers expected that the bills would be paid by their husbands' salaries. This is how marriage worked."

David said, "If you're a man in a marriage today, you can no longer get away with thinking you don't need to chip in with housework. Maybe in the 1950s you could get away with it, but today, it's not a 50 percent contribution from the wife and a 50 percent contribution from the husband. Both parties need to give 100 percent to each other. That's modern marriage."

Men and women today still maintain some traditional roles in modern marriage, but the lines keep blurring. I can point to a number of girlfriends who burn toast and outearn their husbands, just as I know men who are perfectly comfortable in the kitchen and who get up in the night to comfort their crying babies.

How does your relationship fit (or not) into these traditional roles? How do you define "husband"? How do you define "wife"? How do you define marriage?

When Raquel's 89-year-old grandmother visited her and her husband, Matt, in California recently, she was awed by Matt's participation in household chores. She told Raquel that not only did her grandfather not do housework, but "when I had my third child, he didn't even pick me up at the hospital because he was playing baseball. He sent a friend to do it!"

Raquel and I laughed about her comment (really? baseball?), though the image made us sad, too. We thought about how far we've come as wives and women.

Back in my single days, I kept a "must-have" list of qualities I wanted my future husband to possess. While the ability to provide for me was included on that list, my definition of what "providing" meant was quite different from what it meant to my mother. I wanted someone who was financially astute (as she did), but I was also interested in finding a spouse who would support me emotionally and spiritually. I didn't want to settle down unless he was a true partner and unless I felt I could enhance his life as well. Love was one of the most basic ingredients in my matrimony formula.

My friends Mark and Tom, who are in a committed relationship, say they wish they lived in a state where gay marriage is legally sanctioned, not only because they want to combine assets and share the same legal rights as any married couple, but mostly (in Mark's words), "because we love each other and want to express that through the eyes of the law."

Today we choose to marry not because we need to but because we *want* to build a life in partnership with someone we love. This is a major paradigm shift from previous generations.

FEELING UNSETTLED ABOUT SETTLING DOWN

While in some ways the idea of getting married may be more romantic now than ever before, it's also more daunting. When we settle down, we have to reconceive of life as we've come to know it. This has always been the case for people who have merged their lives with someone else; however, by the time we get married these days, most of us have been on our own, outside our parents' homes, for a decade or more. We've grown accustomed to the way we manage our households, our daily routines, and our space. A single 37-year-old woman I once worked with cited "space" as one of the reasons she was worried about sharing her life with another person. She remarked, "I want to get married, but I'm freaking out about sharing my bed with someone. I like having my own home and spreading out around my apartment. . . . I'm worried about giving that up."

It's not just literal physical space that we are concerned about sacrificing in marriage. We also want to have the space to express ourselves and indulge in our own choices without having to check in with someone else for approval. We've become picky and particular about the way we conduct our lives and manage our schedules; the idea of accommodating someone else's needs in our already overbooked lives can be overwhelming to think about. To put it bluntly, we come to marriage somewhat selfish—and happily so.

When my mother married in 1967, the divorce rate in the United States was close to 20 percent (up from 9 percent just a few decades earlier). When I got married 40 years later, the divorce rate had doubled to 40 percent. By 2009, the divorce rate dropped slightly, to 3.4 per 1,000 persons in the population across most of the country; however, we know that couples are less likely to end their marriages during difficult financial times, and these data were collected during a national recession. No matter how we frame it, divorce rates have gone up significantly since our mothers' generation. We tend to inflate the statistic into statements like "50 percent of all marriages fail!" and hold on to that number to rationalize our ambivalence to settle down or use it to explain our fickleness in marriage. Our generation has divorce on the brain.

A therapist I knew once suggested that I consider what my boyfriend would be like if we ever found ourselves in a divorce, advising me, "These days that's an important question to ask yourself before you enter a marriage." She asked me if he'd be diplomatic or difficult, caring or careless.

I don't think you can ever predict how your partner will behave in a divorce, which ranks as one of the most stressful life changes anyone can experience. But I did find it interesting that the counselor thought it was only practical to consider these questions before matrimony.

I'm guessing that many of you grew up with divorced parents or have good friends with divorced parents. If you've been married for a few years, chances are you've already been surprised or upset by a friend's divorce.

It used to be taboo to discuss divorce. Now there are thousands of Web sites, tools, and resources devoted to divorcées. "Divorce parties" are on the rise, with greeting cards and gifts in support of the occasion with messages like "I do. I did. I'm done."

How does the prevalance of divorce affect your marriage? Does it scare you? Inspire you to make sure you and your partner survive?

I asked Katie, a newlywed, if she considered the possibility of divorce before she walked down the aisle. She admitted, "Of course I did! Actually, I obsessed about the decision whether or not to marry my husband because he and I both grew up in broken homes, and I didn't want to go through that again or one day put our children through that. His parents, in particular, had a nasty split. But knowing that we have a greater chance of divorcing because of our backgrounds actually makes us more determined to make our relationship work. We realized we don't have to become victims of our parents' choices."

Another friend, whose parents are divorced, mentioned that every argument she has with her spouse makes her uneasy and contributes to feelings of instability about her marriage. She realizes intellectually that she is not in her mother's marriage, but her parents' divorce prevents her from feeling secure in her own marriage on a daily basis.

In many ways, it's become culturally acceptable to talk about divorce with an almost glib tone. I've heard single male friends joke that they were looking forward to meeting their first wife. Even when we think of the possibility of divorce in serious terms, we are comforted by the idea that there's an option to get out of our marriage should things not "work out." For some of us, that means when significant trust or loyalty has been compromised in our relationships; for others, it means moving on when we are not feeling the same butterflies that initially made us fall in love with our partners.

What does it mean for things to work out? When we exchanged vows that said "for better or for worse," do we really embrace "for worse"? Do we believe that things must organically work out—or that *we* must work them out?

Many would argue that we have lost the stick-to-itiveness that people used to have, both in our marriages and in our everyday lives. In some ways, we are a culture of commitment-phobes. I can relate. I feel a little anxious every time I have to renew my cell-phone contract for another 2 years. What if a better phone or more appealing plan comes out with a different carrier? What if I move to another country and my phone won't work? What if the company goes bankrupt? What if in the next 2 years we'll all be implanted with a chip in our brains and the phone will be obsolete?!

We have short attention spans in many areas of our lives, and our fickleness may cause us to dream up escape routes to leave our marriages rather than dream up exciting new avenues of partnership with the person with whom we decided to share our lives.

INDEBTED TO YOU

One of the biggest causes of divorce is money and financial incompatibility. Whereas many people used to view a prenuptial agreement as a symbol of distrust or potential trouble ahead, many today find it only sensible to enter a legal partnership with a clear economic agreement in case the union doesn't work. I've often said that it's not whether a person has money, but *how* he or she is with money, that daters should look at before they enter a legal long-term partnership.

There's a growing trend for couples to maintain some financial independence in their relationships and not to merge all of their finances upon matrimony. A common financial structure in marriage today is "Yours, Mine, and Ours." In general, Yours, Mine, and Ours bank accounts are organized so that a husband and wife put their salaries in their own individual accounts and allocate a portion of funds each month toward a joint or household account. The partner with the higher income generally contributes a higher percentage of funds to the joint fund each month.

Financial guru Suze Orman recommends that married couples keep individual and joint accounts, including a hefty joint savings account in case one person loses his or her job. She believes couples should contribute to the financial well-being of the home while maintaining their own financial independence, and she argues that these two choices are not mutually exclusive. This approach is certainly a modern money principle. I know that when I told my mother that my husband and I each keep separate accounts for personal purchases, she thought it was odd. If we're a team, she reasoned, why shouldn't everything simply be merged?

Now that couples are marrying later, we are bringing different levels of debt into our relationships, and our money habits are already formed. The Yours, Mine, and Ours financial structure has been shown to alleviate some pressure between couples who have different spending habits (i.e., the spender versus the saver) or couples in which individual credit scores vary.

One couple I spoke with decided to open separate accounts a couple of years into their marriage when they recognized that the husband was regulating everything his wife bought, down to an $8 manicure. She got sick of answering the question "Did you need that?" and decided to put aside money that she earned toward personal purchases. Both of them feel that having separate accounts for little indulgences has helped them avoid built-up resentment.

The decision whether to combine all accounts or hold separate ones is a choice you and your spouse have to make. The approach to structuring your accounts should be managed so that both of your philosophies are honored. There is no correct answer—like anything in marriage, it has to be approached with honesty, communication, and a spirit of compromise.

MAKING MONEY TO MAKING BABIES

Married women find it difficult to achieve a healthy work-life balance today. One cannot give 100 percent to her job, her marriage, and her family and have anything left to give herself. Before settling down, however, a number of us dedicated tremendous time and effort to moving up the career ladder and securing our financial independence. Depending on your career track, you may have occasionally felt out of balance. (I recall a single woman I once coached saying she wanted to marry but had no time to date with her work schedule. I asked her how she would have time to be married if she had no time to date!) Investing all of your time and energy into your career may have been part of your "single" identity. At that time, you were not responsible for anyone but yourself—and you felt good about your achievements. Being compensated for working hard, getting promotions, and spending some of your earnings (your "disposable income") on fantastic experiences or fabulous shoes were gratifying.

Now, in your role as wife and possibly as mother, you may feel disconnected from yourself as the empowered "achiever." I spoke with Marni, married for four years, who stated, "I used to like it when friends joked that I was a workaholic. I know that sounds strange, but I was passionate about my career and I liked the acknowledgment." In her twenties, Marni worked her way up in the PR world and loved the competitive nature of her industry. Now, at 35 years old, she's getting ready to become a mother for the first time and has had to readjust her work schedule to accommodate regular doctor visits, prenatal classes, and her move from the city to the suburbs. She's trying to figure out how long she'll be on maternity leave and how much she'll keep in touch with her colleagues. She admitted that while she is excited to become a mother, she is also worried that she'll be replaced on some of her best accounts when she is out of the office. She also wonders how much time she can take off to adjust to her new role as a mom and how soon she'll have to earn money again, now that she has the financial burden of a mortgage and a new baby. Marni's financial situation is no longer dictated by her wanting to be independent. It's now defined by her realizing others are dependent on her.

How do you reconcile the independent woman you were with the woman you are today?

SCREENING

Walk into the average American household today and you will find a number of screens—TVs, computers, tablets, and cell phones can be found in almost every room. (I'd say perhaps not in the bathroom, but then I think about my friend Matthew who has a flat-screen television by the bathtub and takes his phone into the loo on a regular basis. Like the Fonz, I suppose, he turns the little boy's room into his office.)

Our screen time is not diminishing. You would think our television-viewing habits would decrease with our increased Internet access, but we are watching more television today than we were 10 years ago. In fact, according to a recent Nielsen report, 59 percent of Americans watch TV and surf the Internet simultaneously. And, according to a December 2010 *Wall Street Journal* report, Internet usage is up 121 percent over the past few years. This cannot be helpful to us as we try to date our spouses.

Women like my mother used to complain that their husbands were glued to the tube. Men are still glued, perhaps, but we women have our own intimate relationship with our shows and our screens as well. I'm like Pavlov's dog when my iPhone pings. I race over, with my tail wagging in anticipation, to see who texted, e-mailed, or called or who may have left a witty post on my Facebook page. I tweet close to 10 times a day (I wish that were an exaggeration).

My husband would tell you that I'm more addicted to technology—and all the ways of connecting—than he is. We joke about it now, but we are very aware that this can potentially create a major problem within our marriage. Technology is everywhere around us, and our access to it is only growing. Journalist Bruce Feiler, who examined sleeping arrangements between married couples in a recent *New York Times* article, reported that one in five people is checking Facebook overnight!

After living with a previous boyfriend for 5 years, I had vowed to make a rule of no television or computer in the bedroom in my next relationship. I am so glad I set that boundary. My husband and I can keep the bedroom as a bedroom. Recently, I decided to charge my cell phone in another room at night so I am not checking for messages while in bed (the turning point for me happened when I woke up spooning my cell).

Michael still believes I abuse technology when I exit our room. He thinks we should have a cell-phone basket in the kitchen so we don't pick up our phones during dinner, and he believes we should connect and talk with each other before we turn on the television and get sucked into other peoples' relationships on bad reality TV. He certainly has a point.

The computer is another issue. As someone who works from home, I rarely feel I can switch it off (the computer—or my mind, for that matter). I am constantly working and reworking drafts and answering e-mails. Michael is not technology-free either. Sometimes, I'll tell Michael a highlight of my day and notice that he's completely immersed in cyberspace. It's not like either of us is going to wake up one day and say, "I'm done, honey! I've read every online page!" So we have to create boundaries.

Did you ever imagine you would have to compete with the World Wide Web for your partner's attention? Your usage and dependence on screens won't stop unless you stop it.

The Internet and social networks are not causing affairs (you can't blame a poke on Facebook as the reason you strayed), but the tools are certainly fostering an environment

COMPUTER CLEANSE

In today's frenetic, fast-paced world, there's something counterintuitive but wonderfully calming about being technology-free with no option to check in (or check out, depending on your perspective). The first day you leave technology behind, you will feel jittery and may demonstrate symptoms of withdrawal ("How will anything happen if I don't check in?!"), but by day two, you will reconnect with those around you in a more focused way. It's one of the reasons I secretly appreciate the fact that I can't use my phone (because of crazy roaming fees) in foreign countries.

Challenge: Spend one weekend day this month without any one of your screens. A phone call to make a plan or to check in with a loved one is the exception. See how creative you and your husband become without access to and dependence on technology.

in which it is easier than ever to connect outside your marriage in a discreet way. We'll explore this phenomenon in greater detail in Chapter 6, when we look at infidelity, but it is worth noting that these days we are competing with technology for our partners' attention and affection. Sounds Orwellian, doesn't it?

COMPARISON SHOPPING

It's great to be inspired by the loving union that your parents or grandparents may have had, but comparing your own marriage to theirs isn't fair to you or your relationship. Modern marriage has new rules and different measurements of success.

Do you make decisions in your marriage based on other people's expectations of you? In what ways?

I interviewed a 38-year-old writer named Melanie who said that when her mother began having children, she was 18 years younger than Melanie was when she had her child. When Melanie decided to become a mom, she was at a different life stage and held a job with much different demands and priorities. Melanie has a beautiful little boy and isn't sure she wants more children if she can't provide the very best for them. Her friends understand her position, but her family does not. Her husband's parents say that none of their seven children were deprived of attention or resources growing up—so why not have more?

Melanie reflected on it: "My parents had me 11 months after they got married—that's what you did then. My husband and I wanted to be married for a while before we added a child to the picture. We wanted to make sure we had the resources. The thing is, you think of different things in your early twenties than you do in your late thirties . . . . There's a different level of responsibility. At my stage in life, I feel the burden of doing parenthood 'right' because I'm smarter, calmer, and more focused. I know what I want. Our families may not understand that we are satisfied with having only one child, but we know that we don't want to bring another child into the world unless we can provide for him or her the way we would like to."

Whose life is she going to live? The one set forth by her parents and in-laws, or the one that honors the vision she has created with her husband?

Melanie realizes that her parents and in-laws want what is best for her and her husband; however, they don't always consider the fact that their children are adults, with different values, a different lifestyle, and different needs than their own. Melanie and her husband represent a number of married couples today who are choosing to have smaller families than the ones they grew up in. In some cases, married couples are choosing to have no children. In 2010, the Pew Research Center conducted a survey in conjunction with *Time* magazine about people's views on marriage and family. Eighty-eight percent of respondents considered a married couple without children to be a family.

PEER PRESSURE

One of my girlfriends often feels anxious because she believes that a woman who lives in her neighborhood, who is younger than she is, has "the perfect life": a beautiful big home, two kids, a great body, and an adoring husband. My friend feels like she's failing in some way, as if she and her neighbor are competing on a "Best Wife" reality show. The reality is that my friend has no idea what this woman's life is like behind closed doors. Only the two people in a relationship know how their relationship is working.

We have to stop comparing our marriages and our lives to those of our mothers, friends, and other women. I promise that if you spend your days comparing yourself to others, the other people will win. If I look for her, I can always find someone prettier, thinner, richer, and happier than I am. It is an exhausting exercise.

Rather than comparing yourself to other women from another era or from another area of town, consider using yourself as a frame of reference. Are you measuring up to the vision you held when you relinquished your single status and decided to merge lives with your husband? What kind of partner did you want to be? What kind of woman did you want to be?

Marriage—and our expectations around marriage—looks different today than it did in past generations. We want to be supported as much as we want to be expressed. And with the competing demands for our attention, we have to choose to consciously create space for connecting with our spouses every day.

Our lives may seem bigger and fuller than ever before, but here's one thing that all couples I spoke with mentioned: It's the little things that determine whether you enjoy your marriage or feel disconnected from it. The most important gift you can give to any of your relationships, and especially your marriage, is your presence.

Recently, over lunch, my 80-year-old friend Carol remarked, "Today's generation tries to connect by buying stuff and trying to impress. There's too much ego. People don't need that. They need you."

She added one more piece of advice before we left. "Don't get so distracted and don't be so distraught about your future. Today is an exciting time to be married and to be a woman! Enjoy your life and enjoy your relationships while you can. Make your marriage a priority. Otherwise, why the heck did you give up your singlehood and settle down?"

She raised an excellent question.

WIVES' TALE
The Perfect Wife

NAME: Sara
AGE: 28
MARRIED: 1 year
CHILDREN: No

Scenario

Sara has seen friends' and families' marriages fall apart and has decided that for her marriage to last, she must be dedicated to being the "perfect" wife. She is the consummate homemaker—the house is always clean, she is fastidious about each room's decor, and she provides a delicious homemade dinner almost every night as part of her domestic routine. She is highly self-controlled and disciplined and works hard to maintain her weight and physical appearance, but she never feels that she has done anything well enough.

Sara is a perfectionist not only with herself but also with her husband. Patience is not one of her virtues, and when she feels things are out of order, she is quick to judge those around her. The more impatient Sara becomes with herself, the more she views her husband as lazy or unthoughtful.

Issue

Sara wants a perfect home and a perfect life, but no such thing exists. She must recognize that she cannot have true intimacy without vulnerability. If she wants to have a successful relationship, she needs to be more present and flexible and learn to let go of her need to be in control at all times.

Sara might think, "Why is it up to me to get everything done right around here?" and not realize how self-defeating and exhausting this approach can be. She is bound to have a breakdown if she continues to put so much pressure on herself, and she is likely to alienate her husband, who can't possibly satisfy her goals of perfection.

Sara may place great value on organizing the silverware or folding the laundry a certain way, but her husband may not want to spend his energy on something he considers to be a waste of time. The more Sara tries to impose her way of doing things and organizing the home (and her life) on her partner, the more irritable she will get with him for failing to meet her standards, and the less interested he will be in pleasing his wife.

Solution

Sara must learn that it is okay to ask for help, defer to her partner for his ideas, and show her vulnerability. She must recognize that the goal of being perfect is, in itself, imperfect and flawed. She also must remember that great lessons exist for her in the imperfect parts of her relationship and life—this is where real learning and growth can occur.

Sara needs to become conscious and aware of her inner judgments so she can see how they are holding her back in some areas of her life. While she should not abandon her value of being principled and organized, qualities that are inherent to her character, she should identify when she goes too far in voicing her criticisms and learn to edit her complaints.

Journal

For 1 week, Sara should record each time she feels uptight about the way her husband does something, judgmental about something a loved one said, or critical about something she has done that she does not perceive to be good enough. Once she reviews her list, she will likely see a theme and realize how many hot buttons she has. Picking battles in life is integral to having successful relationships with others and with oneself. Seeing this in writing may be a wake-up call.

Get Messy!

Sara should practice being present rather than focusing on the external things around her. Whenever an uncomfortable feeling arises, instead of immediately jumping into action to fix it, Sara should sit with her feeling and recognize that it is okay to feel sad or anxious. (If she doesn't, her feeling will fester and manifest in another, much messier, way.)

Physical messiness in her home makes Sara feel out of control. For a weekend, Sara should not clean up after her spouse and let him run the home without her direction. She may see that the world will not collapse without everything being lined up at all times.

CHAPTER THREE

Turn ME On

What makes the engine go? Desire, desire, desire.
—Stanley Kunitz

It's inevitable. Wedding vows, anniversary speeches, and Valentine's Day cards include Jerry Maguire's line, often cited as one of the most romantic movie moments, "You complete me."

I'm certain that every day, couples all across America exchange these three words with a sense of confidence and comfort. There is a feeling that *this* is how marriage should be: You are complete once you have found your other half.

The idea of one person completing another person dates back to the Bible, after all. Eve was created from Adam's rib, and the two beings were thus intrinsically linked. Thousands of years later, Plato shared the sentiment of two halves becoming whole in his dialogue *Symposium*. He wrote, "Each of us when separated, having one side only, like a flat fish, is but the indenture of a man, and he is always looking for his other half." The idea was that man would spend his entire life yearning and searching for this half to complete him.

A bride-to-be once called me for advice because she was concerned that she didn't look at her future husband as her "everything." She told me she loved her fiancé immensely and was excited to build a life with him and start a family together. But she also said that she valued her independence and enjoyed her life, and she was terrified of giving that up. She didn't want to lose herself in her marriage in order to merge into "one." She wondered if it was possible to put her marriage first while making her own needs a priority. I assured her that she had a healthy perspective and that I would be concerned if she thought of her impending marriage in any other way.

"You complete me" is not my definition of what finding a soul mate looks like. When I hear people say those words, or some version of them, I have a burning desire to pull a Tom Cruise (circa 2005) by jumping on the nearest couch and exclaiming, "*Nobody* completes you! Be complete, be whole, be happy! That's the best formula you can have for a healthy partnership!"

I assure you, I love *love*. I love the idea of becoming a better person when you are with a good partner. There is no doubt that a good mate can bring out your best qualities and help you reach your highest potential. In fact, that's my definition of a "soul mate." Rather than losing your identity to a relationship, or feeling incomplete without another person in your life, being with the right partner can help you grow and evolve into an even more authentic version of yourself.

So maybe the better version of Jerry's infamous line is "You *complement* me" or "You make my already wonderful life so much richer." When you know this (and really believe it), you approach your relationship with yourself and your spouse differently. You have a strong sense of your role in your marriage and outside it, and you aren't likely to assign solely your husband the task of making you happy. As 80-year-old Carol notes, "I wish women wouldn't wait for men to rescue them. That's an antiquated idea. Nobody can provide your happiness but you."

Carol has been widowed twice, and she thanks both of her husbands for teaching her so much about herself. Like many in her generation, she married young, but she realized early on that she had to have her own creative, fulfilling outlets outside her marriage to truly enjoy her life. Neither of her partners was threatened by this need. In fact, Carol's passion for life was one of the qualities they most admired about her.

When she met her first husband, Carol was a dancer. Dancing was always one of her greatest joys, so in the early years of her marriage she followed her dream to open a dance studio. When she eventually moved on from her dance studio years later, she asked herself again, "What do I love to do and how can I do it?" Then she created her next business, designing jewelry. She even named her company "ME Inc.," as she never took being a self-expressed woman for granted.

One common theme that came up time and again among women who told me they were happily married was that they were all *happy* in general. They maintain their own interests and goals outside their marriages, and they have a strong, positive sense of who they are as women in addition to being wives.

EXPRESS YOURSELF

Too many of us women feel selfish when we do things for ourselves. There's pressure to balance it all—raising kids, creating a nice home, excelling at work, having a great marriage, and looking fabulous the whole time.

That guilt for honoring oneself is sometimes demonstrated by apologies. Linguist Deborah Tannen has studied communication patterns of men and women and says that women, who apologize more frequently than men, are taking away their power when they say "sorry" for every little thing.

Women say "sorry" a lot—to each other, when we ask for something we know we need and in my case, to the table leg I kicked at dinner the other night. Some of us have a hard time saying or even knowing what we *want*.

Being bratty and selfish, so that you never consider others, is certainly not a good quality, but being focused on your needs is essential to your happiness—and to the happiness of the people you live with.

One of my friends from college, a busy mother of two, says she feels too guilty to get a haircut, to go out with girlfriends, or to pursue any of her own interests. "My family needs me more than I need those things," she tells me, half convincingly. She's tired. She feels the blahs in her marriage and says she's bored by her job and doesn't like her neighbors. Her husband told me that he wishes she would get out of the house more and reconnect with her old friends. He doesn't want the perfect wife—he wants a happy one.

I don't recognize my friend lately, and I don't think she recognizes herself either. Sure, our priorities shift as we travel through adulthood and parenthood, but we don't want to create a recipe for a midlife crisis or set ourselves up for straying outside marriage just because we need to feel excited and connected again. If my friend continues down the path she's on, she will likely get off track in one way or another. Her lack of attention to herself will not benefit her, her husband, or her family.

Our self-expression as women transcends our responsibilities as wives and mothers.

Whether we're married or single, we all want to be appreciated for the many qualities and talents we possess. This may not have been as much of a priority in past generations, even though women undoubtedly craved self-fulfillment then, too.

So what are you passionate about? What would your ME Inc. company be?

If nothing immediately comes to mind, consider this question: If time and resources were not an issue, how would you spend your days? Is there anything you used to do before marriage (other than pick up men!) that you wish was a part of your life today?

These are essential questions to ask yourself as you travel through marriage. It's easy to lose yourself in the many demands of matrimony and motherhood. Too many women wake up years into marriage and wonder if they're living the lives they're meant to have.

Of course, when you decide to become a parent, your children become your biggest priority. Part of parenting is recognizing your family's needs and making sure they are cared for. My parents always ensured I had access to things they didn't have growing up. But you can't properly care for your family if you are not taking care of yourself. If your mother didn't eat when you were in her womb, you would not have survived. If you grew up watching your parents' relationship deteriorate, or sensing your mother's unhappiness, you wouldn't have felt secure. Parents can't give their children a happy life if they ignore themselves in the process. Your duty is to make sure your children are protected and your husband is supported, and part of the way you do this is by honoring your own needs. Every successful relationship starts with the relationship you have with yourself.

IT'S NEVER TOO LATE TO FIND YOURSELF

I have a friend who has wanted to be a psychologist since she was in high school. When she was 36 years old, she was on the fence—should she follow her dream and invest time and money to go back to school, or should she stay in her current job, which she didn't really like but was stable? She was married and settled in her life. Why rock the boat? "Besides," she once told me, "I wouldn't be able to do anything with the training until I'm at least 40, and that's a little old to be starting again, don't you think?"

Six years later, my friend is still figuring out what she wants to be when she grows up (her words). She recently admitted,

"I'm 42 and in the same position I was in a few years ago, feeling like I need to find a job I care about—except this time I have a little more gray in my hair."

She now realizes she would be 42 years old even if she had earned her credentials in psychology, so she may as well have followed her passion.

That's the thing about decisions—whether or not you make them, life continues. You have to ask yourself what you are willing to give up to make the choice or what you are willing to lose if you don't.

One way to help you make these decisions is to create a cost-benefit analysis to help you see more clearly how your life can benefit from taking a risk. I asked my friend to do a cost-benefit analysis about going back to school at age 36:

Cost:

Time: Years of taking courses, homework, will be over 40 when done.

Money: Classes, textbooks.

Benefit: New knowledge and skills, ability to potentially work for myself, generate new revenue source. I'd be more fulfilled in my life and, ultimately, my marriage, because I'd be doing something I really cared about. I'd be following my dream (priceless).

Many women have goals outside their careers, of course. I once had a client who struggled with speaking up for herself. Instead of focusing on how to handle people who took advantage of her, we decided to focus on her secret dream to be a femme fatale. We set a goal for her to start taking martial arts classes, which would help build her confidence and fulfill her secret butt-kicking fantasy. I asked her, "Would you prefer to cross it

off some bucket list when you're older and perhaps not as physically fit, or would you rather learn the moves now?"

Twelve Tuesdays later, she gained a ribbon and lost pounds.
Her husband and children barely recognized the new, energetic,
confident wife and mom they had. Even more amazing is that
she recognized herself more than she had in ages—not because
she was kicking butt now, but because she realized she hadn't
been that energetic person for so many years. She had lost her
sense of self and her confidence when she put everybody else's
needs before her own. Now, she felt like a superhero.

I recently asked her husband how the martial arts hobby
affected their relationship. "No question," he said, "she's sexier
and stronger. It's less about the way her body's changed and
more about her attitude."

This is how my client's cost-benefit sheet looks now:

Cost:

Time: Tuesday nights, time away from the kids.

Money: Classes, gas, gear.

Benefit: More energy and enthusiasm for the rest of the week,
   more toned body, happier, new skill, can defend myself in a
   dangerous situation, new girlfriends/class buddies, better
   relationships since I speak up more, closer with my husband
   (emotionally and physically).

GET PASSIONATE ABOUT YOUR LIFE

Too many married women don't recognize the sexy, sassy,
sophisticated women they were when they were single—and
they miss this aspect of themselves.

When was the last time you really *wanted* something (not
someone)—when you felt so giddy with excitement or so driven

to achieve it that you closed your eyes and dreamed about it and woke up thinking about it?

Remember Raquel, who swooned over her future husband, Matt, when they first met? Whereas she used to feel butterflies and see sparkles when she looked at Matt, she now admitted, "I would give anything to feel any kind of desire. Not only in my marriage, but in my life."

Raquel is onto something. Desire for her husband has to be sparked first by a general feeling of *desire*.

I knew Raquel in San Francisco almost a decade ago when she was curating sensual photography exhibits. I was immediately drawn to her at the party where we met because she was engaging, comfortable in her own skin, and vibrant. Raquel oozed spice and sass in those days, and her passion and playfulness were apparent. She radiated a wonderful confidence and joie de vivre at her shows and, in fact, met her husband at one of them.

Raquel used to lead "Goddess Groups" where she empowered women to find and express their inner goddess. She was passionate about helping women connect to their power and sensuality and to find play in their busy lives. Now that she's gained a little postbaby weight and has chosen to stay at home with her daughter, her only real play is, well, child's play. Raquel has a beautiful baby girl and is fulfilled as a mother. Her daughter is her pride and joy. Is that enough to fulfill her? Sometimes. And when it isn't, she—like many other mothers—often feels guilty.

She reflected on it: "In any creative endeavor, even if it's your passion, you have to make a commitment to it and have the energy to make it happen. You have to consider things like: How am I going to do it, what is it going to look like, who will I leave my baby with? It's not that I can't do these things, but I'm feeling disconnected and probably a little lazy. After quitting my old career, I went into a different state. My life has tremendous purpose now that I'm a mom, but do I recognize myself? Not really."

Raquel was invited to a friend's party recently on a Saturday night. She knew she would have reconnected with some girl-friends she misses if she attended, but at the time she felt it was easier to stay in. "My husband would have watched our daughter, so I can't even use that as an excuse," she admitted. In many ways, she feels out of the loop and is nervous to get back in the game of life. She's forgotten that reengaging in activities that make her happy doesn't require abandoning the rest of her responsibilities. Like many of us who are juggling responsibilities, Raquel has convinced herself, her husband, and her friends that she's not socializing with them because of all of her commitments, but the reality is that Raquel is scared to reengage in her life. It is easier to hide than to take action.

Raquel is stuck. "I feel like my legs are in mud," she explained. It takes energy to climb out of the mud, but she knows she has to make that climb if she wants to enjoy her life and her marriage. "I owe it not only to myself, but to my relationship. I don't even want to be with me," she admitted. "The funny thing is that anytime I haven't felt like going to a party, taking a vacation, or tapping into my creativity and I've done it anyway, I've gotten more energy just by doing it," she added.

Sometimes, we don't think we have energy to do the things that bring us pleasure; we forget that once we take action, it often creates the very energy we were lacking. We get our spark back not only by dreaming about our desires, but by doing what is necessary to achieve them.

I reminded Raquel of what drew me to her as my friend and how I've always admired her infectious spunk and passion. During our conversation, I could hear Raquel perking up on the other end of the phone, as if she was thinking, "Yes—that *is* me! You see me! Where did I go?"

We talked about the small steps she can take toward getting her old self back. She can go shopping with a girlfriend to boost her confidence (she laughed about the fact that her daughter sports beautiful clothes while she wears shoes with holes in them) or join a friend for a creative brainstorming session at lunch. She may head to a local park with her camera for a few hours to reconnect with her love of photography. The list went on.

And that's the great thing about desire: It's like smelling delicious food when you don't even realize you're hungry. Desire is in each of us. When it has been turned off or lost, we forget how much it feeds us. Talking about, dreaming about, and doing the things that are meaningful to us remind us that passion is still there. In fact, it has always been there.

Is there a hobby or activity that you used to enjoy that you haven't done in a long time? What has stopped you?

Last year, I heard *Project Runway* star Tim Gunn talk about his rise to fame as a middle-aged man. Gunn worked at Parsons the New School for Design for 23 years before a television network reached out to him to consult for a new fashion competition show in development. He's now one of the most recognizable faces on TV. In the interview, Gunn described how surreal it is to be considered a "star" and said he pinches himself frequently. In his fifties, he's at the pinnacle of his career, and new opportunities are pouring in.

I'm not suggesting that you star in a reality show or radically alter your schedule and your lifestyle. One key of happiness is to find balance and recognize that making a change does not require an all-or-nothing mentality. Seeing your life through a black-or-white lens can be counterproductive to reaching your goals, in fact. Big leaps in personal fulfillment are often made with small steps toward your wants.

Think back to one of your seminal experiences—a time in your life when you felt most yourself, confident, and connected to your wants. What were you doing? How can you incorporate some of those elements into your life? (*Note:* If your peak experience was climbing Machu Picchu, you don't need to fly back to Peru, but you may realize that you love physical challenges and adventure and decide to reengage in activities, like hiking, that bring you back to your passion.)

WHO HAS TIME FOR SELF-EXPRESSION?

Most of us strive for balance. But these days, when we're working longer hours, spending more time engaging with technology, and supersizing our lives, who has time for balance?

I recently realized I needed an assistant, but I couldn't get my act together to hire one. The issue was that I needed an intern to hire the assistant. (Which begged the question: Who, then, will hire the intern?!)

We're all familiar with public health campaigns that urge us to eat a "balanced diet," but how many of us have a well-balanced *life diet* that includes fun, work, social and family connections, good health, and more?

Think of your life as a delicious (albeit large) pie. In your pie, you may have eight slices, each with different flavors. Some flavors are sweet and some are sour. Your slices may include Career, Health, Significant Other, Fun, Money, Friends and Family, Personal Growth, and Physical Environment.

Career: Do you enjoy your job? Does it align with the career path you want? Are you fulfilled?

Health: Are you maintaining a healthy body weight? Are you eating well and working out regularly? Are there any health issues that you need to attend to?

Significant Other: Are you and your spouse giving each other the support and love that you would like? Are there any frustrations or resentments you have to tackle?

Fun: Are you engaged in fun activities outside home or work? Do you have creative outlets? Do you and your husband have fun together? Do you struggle to remember the last time you laughed?

Money: Do you feel anxious or comfortable when you think about money? Have you ignored bills, or are you on top of your finances? Are you satisfied with the income you and/or your spouse bring in to maintain your lifestyle?

Friends and Family: Do you have healthy relationships with your friends and family? Would you like to see friends and family more (or less)? Is there any member of your family or a friend with whom you have to resolve issues?

Personal Growth: Are you conscious of your needs and wants? Do you listen to your gut or ignore it in favor of other peoples' needs?

Physical Environment: Are you comfortable and happy in your home? Is there any area of your home that needs organizing or repair? Are you happy in your neighborhood and city?

On a scale of 1 to 10, how good do you feel about each aspect of your life pie? Placing a rating of 8 under Money, for instance, doesn't necessarily mean you have a lot of money in the bank. Rather, 8 would indicate that you feel very good about your relationship with your money and are satisfied with your financial state. When you think of Fun, you might rank it a 3 if you can barely recall the last time you had a fun day or night. If you have to think too hard about fun, I'm guessing you haven't experienced it lately.

Take out a piece of paper and rank each slice of your pie from 1 to 10. What does your pie reveal? Are there areas of the pie you're currently neglecting? Where do you need to put more effort so you can have a well-balanced life diet?

As a second step, write two actions you can take under each category that would bring your score up by at least a point. For instance, if you ranked Physical Environment low, think of two things you can do to raise your number. You may write, "Get the dishwasher repaired" or "Give away clothes I'm not wearing so I can organize my closet."

You'll start to notice that all of the pieces of your life pie work together. When one is out of sync, the others are usually thrown off course, too.

The third step is to choose a date as your benchmark for each action, so that you are accountable to your goals. Enlist a family member or friend to report to. If that's impossible, set reminders on your computer or phone so that you are sticking to your "by when" schedule.

Your last step is to JUST DO IT!

Of course, this exercise is simple to sketch out on paper and much harder to implement in your life, but if you want to find balance, you have to consciously create it. You may have to say no to certain commitments so you can say yes to others that you value more.

If your life were as good as it could get, what would that look like? If it were twice as good, what picture would you see?

ME-CATIONS

According to research released by the American Resort Development Association, 38 percent of women polled, particularly women in their thirties and forties, are choosing to take vacations without their families. And the trend is growing each year.

More and more married women are taking *me*-cations— traveling solo or with girlfriends to destinations that appeal to them (or staying close to home on their own mini-sabbaticals) to recharge without their significant others or kids.

Many of these women say they return from their getaways happier and more focused on their families. The boost they get from a vacation without their significant others or children is surprisingly effective. In fact, bonding with female friends in particular is good for their mental and emotional health. When women feel close to a girlfriend, their progesterone levels increase, helping to boost mood and alleviate stress.

I used to perform in high school plays with my friend Lisa, who was a free spirit like me. Happily married now, she works hard to create a balance between making marriage a priority and being expressed as an individual.

"My marriage is a top priority, and my husband, Mark, knows that, but my marriage works best when I have interests outside of it," Lisa said. She has never felt that she had to give up who she is to be a good wife to Mark.

She recalled one of the best weekends she had experienced in her 12-year marriage. She went to Manhattan by herself over a long weekend to see half a dozen plays that she was "dying to see." Her husband is not a theater buff and couldn't get the time off of work, so she went to New York City on her own. Lisa wasn't leaving any big responsibilities at home and didn't feel guilty about heading on a mini-vacation. In fact, she felt empowered and energized by the experience. In a way, taking the trip renewed her commitment to her husband. She realized she could be loyal to him and loyal to her own needs—the two were not mutually exclusive.

"I had the best time on my trip to New York," Lisa recalled. "Mark and I kept in touch often, and he was so happy for me that I got to go and blow off steam, as I had been working crazy hours for 5 months. He knew it was something I was so excited about, and even though he didn't go, he loved to hear me talk about it because I was so passionate about it. I saw five shows in 4 days and had a blast. When I landed at the airport back in Toronto, Mark was waiting for me and we were both excited. My excitement continued at home."

Lisa thinks of her New York theatre weekend getaway as a turning point in her marriage because she realized that nurturing her creativity was essential to her happiness and could therefore make her relationship even stronger. Mark also has interests he explores without her. He loves to go boating and fishing and will occasionally take trips out of town with his buddies. Lisa supports and encourages him to explore his interests. She believes that their support of each other's passions only makes their connection stronger.

The Sari-cation

I recently called my friend Matt, who mentioned that he was taking his two children to California to visit his parents while his wife, Sari, would be on her annual Sari-cation.

For those of you who haven't seen this vacation advertised . . . .

Sari-cation: A chance for Sari—a mom of two young boys, an executive at a Fortune 50 company, and the driving force

behind her booming business called BooginHead that she runs
on the side (the side of what, I don't know, as I don't understand how she has time for it all)—to unplug from all of her
duties for a week. (Whew! Even writing that sentence felt
exhausting.)

During the Sari-cation, Sari can visit with friends, head
out on minitrips, go to the gym, and take over the house. She
might decide to watch endless hours of bad reality television
on her TiVo and gab on the phone, or eat ice cream for dinner
and sleep until noon. She has few responsibilities for a full
week out of the year. In essence, the Sari-cation is Matt's
annual gift to his wife so that she can reconnect with herself
and recharge.

Matt said, "I tell her not to feel guilty about taking the time
off from us. Certain people don't need or want that time to
unplug, but my wife loves it, and it makes me happy to see her
so happy. She works her tail off, and this week provides a little
weight lifted off her back. She's bringing in a lot to this house.
She's driven for the betterment of our family. It's the week to
regenerate the soul."

If you think Sari's husband is an enlightened and generous
man, well . . . you would be correct. He would tell you, though,
that it's not just an act of selflessness on his part.

"The reward is multiple for me," Matt admitted. "Giving my
wife this opportunity is better for her and better for our family.
When we see her after the week, everyone is excited. As an
added bonus, I have special memories with the boys during the
week apart. We all win."

I told my friend Melanie about the getaway. Melanie is a
38-year-old mother of a 2-year-old son, and she works for the
relationship site YourTango.com. I asked if she had any desire
to take a *Melanie*-cation. She mentioned that she recently
attended a conference out of state, and it was the first time she
had left her husband and son alone.

"I was guilt-ridden on the first day and couldn't stop thinking about them," she said. "But by day two and three, I had adjusted and was feeling good. I was walking differently and smiling a lot. I started to feel like myself again."

I asked Melanie if she realized she hadn't felt like herself in a couple of years, and she admitted that she didn't even recognize that she was missing part of who she is because she loved putting everything into her son, Oliver. Over the 2 years since becoming a mother, she had stopped seeing girlfriends, reading books, writing, taking hot baths, and treating herself to little indulgences that were some of her favorite things when she was single. She lost a piece of herself so she could assume the role of wife and mother. Melanie thinks of the conference as a great lesson that she is thankful to have learned relatively early on in her marriage.

"I see how important it is to get away from your marriage or your duties as a parent every so often so you can reconnect with yourself. I like the definition of who I am, and when I'm able to connect with others and come back to my marriage, my sex life and communication are better. My husband remembers who he fell in love with."

The benefit to Melanie's marriage was amazing, and her getaway was a positive bonding experience for her husband and son. When she left for the conference weekend, her son was counting to two; when she returned, he could count to 10. "My husband was bragging about being superdad!" she joked. She was more attracted to her husband than she had been in months.

Melanie is planning to go away again this winter. She observed: "I was good at the self-expression piece of my life before, and once I had a kid, I forgot the importance and benefit of it."

Lisa, Sari, and Melanie are not disloyal or unique wives for craving some time away from all of their other duties. In fact, more and more women I speak with crave outlets outside their marriages and away from mommyhood so they can remember who they are. Some are better at finding it (rather, creating it) than others.

WHAT ABOUT HIS PASSIONS?

There's a stereotype that when men get married, they have to give up time with their friends and sacrifice fun. How many times have you heard a groom being told to enjoy his "last day of freedom"? Unfortunately, some women perpetuate this idea and feel threatened when their husbands have fun without them.

I spoke with Jodi, who feels excluded when her husband enjoys outings with friends. "He plays tennis a few times a month and doesn't ask me to join," she said. A moment later, she told me she doesn't play tennis very well but hates to be left out. I asked her what she does well, and she paused and reflected. "I used to be good at art, but now, not really . . . . I don't know . . . ." She folded her arms in frustration. Her husband is frustrated, too. He mentioned to me, privately, that he occasionally sneaks out to see his buddies so he won't get into an argument with his wife. Deceit as a requirement to have fun? This pattern can't be good for their marriage.

It seems strange that any of us wouldn't want to support and nurture our husbands' hobbies considering that we were initially attracted to the fact that they had passions, social outlets, and interests besides us. Let's face it, would any of us marry men who were needy of our attention every day and had no friends or hobbies?

The male equivalent of the me-cation—man-cations—are also on the rise, though they are not as popular as girlfriend getaways. TripAdvisor.com reported a 7 percent increase in the number of men traveling with male friends in 2010 compared to 2009.

Dolores, who has been married to David for 37 years, believes in giving her husband time and space to engage in his interests. David doesn't take for granted the fact that his wife has always encouraged him to spend time with his friends and go fishing, even while their kids were young. He said, "We had one car, and Dolores knew the boys' weekend was important to me, so she always gave me the car for that."

While David was telling me what a lucky guy he is to have such a supportive wife, Dolores interrupted him to tell me that her husband has also gone out of his way to make sure her needs are met. When she was a teacher and hosted school functions at the house, David would clean the house and stay out of the way. David and Dolores spent most of their time together, but on the days when they saw friends separately, they encouraged the other to "Go have fun!" and they always meant it. Their trips never included a guilt trip.

Dolores said, "The interesting thing about marriage is that when you do things for each other, and let your partner enjoy his or her friends and interests, you will get the same respect. David and I did a lot together when we were raising our children, but we weren't threatened by our differences. We realized those things also needed to be expressed."

Being in a relationship means being sensitive not only to your need for self-expression but also to your partner's need to be fulfilled. What are his dreams? Is he acting on them? Are you supporting and encouraging him to be expressive, or are you threatened by interests that don't include you?

Melanie was so recharged by her out-of-state conference experience a few months ago that she told her husband to find a program he was interested in attending and sign up for it immediately. She wanted him to experience what it was like to step away from his family duties. He found something to attend that would last only a day, and Melanie encouraged him to go away for longer than a night. "Go for four nights!" she told him. She admitted that in addition to wanting to give her husband the gift of time away like she had, she also wanted to experience some bonding time with her son. She says now that a me-cation will likely become a part of their marriage, and one that should only strengthen it.

A GOOD WE STARTS WITH A GOOD ME

Many of you may feel like you are running an endless and exhausting marathon, with few opportunities to catch your breath. When you're married, and possibly a parent, your schedule is demanding, and other people depend on you. It's unrealistic to expect that your life will look the same as it did before marriage or that life will always feel exciting, but you should still be able to recognize yourself and the core values and passions that you expressed in your life before you took on the roles of wife and mother.

When you are engaged in pursuits that have value and meaning to you, your fulfillment and happiness will carry over into your marriage. Be complete—with no apologies.

WIVES' TALE

The Mommy Martyr

NAME: Kate
AGE: 34 years old
MARRIED: 9 years
CHILDREN: 4 and 6 years old

Scenario

Kate puts everybody's needs—her husband's, children's, in-laws', friends', co-workers'—before her own. She feels that to be a good mother, wife, and member of society, she must always give priority to others. She genuinely enjoys doing things for her family and friends, and being generous is part of her identity. In fact, when she's not going out of her way to please others, Kate feels less important and inauthentic. She identifies herself as a nurturer and likes to be needed.

Although she doesn't do things for the praise, she feels hurt when people don't notice her efforts. She bites her tongue when her in-laws or kids and spouse make demands on her. (For instance, if she cooks a nice meal for her family and they complain, she will throw it out and let them choose anything they want her to make.) Almost a decade into her marriage Kate feels overwhelmed by everyone's demands and constantly feels underappreciated.

Issue

Kate doesn't feel anybody reciprocates her attention or looks out for her needs (though she rarely verbalizes them, she wishes people noticed). She continues to juggle all of her responsibilities at home and at work and expects people to be grateful and return some of the favors. The more people in her life don't show respect or gratitude for her hard work and thoughtfulness, the more Kate feels resentment creep up. Kate generally looks on the bright side and chooses to ignore uncomfortable feelings of resentment, so her frustration manifests in other ways.

Kate's husband feels that his wife is passive-aggressive and wishes she would be more direct when she wants to share something that is important to her. He finds it difficult to understand his wife's needs—perhaps because she rarely asks for what she needs—and feels that he must constantly anticipate her wants. For him, the process is tiring. He can tell Kate is frustrated and rundown and wishes she would take better care of herself. He wants her to indulge more in things that would make her happy rather than spend every day making others happy.

Solution

Kate has to get over the idea that putting attention on her needs will drive others away. In fact, she will create more authentic relationships if she learns to *ask* for her wants. Being generous and selfless are wonderful qualities, but not if they are at the expense of Kate's own comfort and happiness. She must remember that she cannot have a true connection with her partner if she hides her needs (or if she communicates her needs in manipulative ways). Her need to be needed creates tension with some family members. She must learn that people will still love and appreciate her even when she does things for herself and asserts what she wants.

Checklist

Kate should put together a list at the start of each day of what she wants or needs to do *for herself*—and stick to it! This means she may need to delegate some tasks. If she doesn't learn to allow other people to help her, she will burn out. Kate must embrace the idea of *boundaries* and practice setting a few each week. So, if her colleagues at work expect her to finish a task that is not within the realm of her responsibilities, or if her kids won't listen, she must learn not to acquiesce.

Time Out

When the instinct to please people arises, Kate should take a moment and ask herself what she wants and if the people calling her for help really *need* her or just expect her to pitch in because she's *good old reliable Kate.*

When she feels guilty for not rushing to take care of everything for her husband and children, she must recognize that letting them do a few things on their own will be good for their character. If she babies her family too much, she may be enabling bad behavior later.

CHAPTER FOUR

Words, Words, Words

My friend Mariana's Russian mother gave her profound advice before she got married. She told Mariana, "Never initiate an important discussion with your husband if he is hungry or tired. Make sure to give him something to eat before talking."

I used to chuckle at her mother's tip, and now I think of it often. The reality is that without a nap and a snack, Michael and I can behave like children during an argument (or, more accurately, a disagreement may be sparked *because* we haven't had adequate rest or eaten yet).

These days, anytime I want to discuss something important with my husband, I do a mental check. Has he eaten recently? Check! Is he awake enough to hear me now? Check! Timing is everything when broaching significant topics.

Of course, sometimes you don't know you're about to have a heavy conversation, and seemingly out of the blue, a casual chat becomes a significant *talk*. You can't always throw rest or a meal into the equation. You have to trust that you and your partner have the tools to communicate effectively.

Relationship experts and counselors put a lot of stock in a couple's communication skills. Studies show that the health of a marriage can be predicted simply by observing how a couple negotiates and discusses even the little things. Do they listen to each other? Are they secretive or open? Do they use negative language? What does their body language demonstrate?

DATE TALK

Chances are communication was effortless when you and your future spouse were dating. You and he could talk to one another until the sun came up, and you may have felt that neither of you would ever tire of listening to the other. (You didn't realize, of course, that your dopamine high was contributing to your conversation marathons!) In those days, conversations with your man were sweet and interesting—and so were you. Your husband may not have agreed with everything you said (and when he didn't agree, your conversations were lively), but you knew he essentially cared about what you had to say. You appreciated his way of seeing the world as well. You were curious to hear his perspective.

The average single woman I've interviewed won't go out with someone again if he is a poor listener. In fact, the number-one complaint both men and women share on a first date is that their date talked too much and didn't pay attention to them. This finding isn't surprising, as it follows one of the most basic relationship principles—that people want to be seen and heard (and ultimately valued) for who they are.

We know that healthy communication is the cornerstone of a happy relationship, yet it is something that inevitably suffers when schedules are hectic or we become too comfortable (read: lazy) to pay attention to the words we choose. Without committing to conscious communication in our relationship, we cannot hope to bring back the fun and excitement that our relationship once enjoyed.

HOW DO YOU COMMUNICATE WITH YOUR SPOUSE?

Imagine you're pulling into the driveway of your home after a long day—one of those days when all you want to do is crawl into bed the moment you walk inside and forget that you have responsibilities to anybody else. Work was a headache and traffic was horrible. You are hungry, tired, and irritated. You don't feel like acting like an adult; you just want to mope around. You open your front door and are greeted by your spouse, who says, "I shouldn't have relied on you tonight. You never help out around here!"

How would you react? Do you think you would hear the complaint and respond to it effectively? This is the scenario my friend Bill described to me recently when he recounted a big fight he had with his wife.

Psychologist and mathematician Dr. John Gottman has been examining and collecting data on married couples for more than 2 decades. I think of him as the "divorce whisperer" because he can predict, with approximately 90 to 98 percent accuracy, whether or not a couple will survive their marriage by watching them interact for less than an hour. In fact, he's gotten his test down to such an exact science that he can determine much about a couple's communication style and compatibility in just a few minutes. Dr. Gottman has identified some of the warning signs that a couple, even an ostensibly happy one, may be headed for divorce down the road.

The way you begin an argument with your partner can predict how it will end. A "harsh start-up," which involves leading your complaint with criticism, is the first warning sign that a couple does not communicate in a healthy manner, according to Dr. Gottman. Not surprisingly, a discussion that starts out negatively or with an attack on your spouse's character is unlikely to reach a resolution.

Bill's wife had a reasonable complaint the night they got into a fight. She had a frustrating day trying to get work done at home while taking care of their kids' needs. With a child in daycare and a baby at home, she wasn't able to check off half of the items on her to-do list. These days, she barely has time to meet her deadlines, and her work is suffering as a result. Like her husband, she had a stressful day. Her complaint that Bill didn't call to mention he would be late for dinner, even after he promised he would help out, is a pattern that throws off the family's schedule. When the family's schedule is out of balance, the children's sleep schedule is affected, too—and this contributes to more crankiness for all. There is nothing inherently argumentative about Bill's wife's complaint; kids need schedules, and spouses need to think about each other when planning meals and activities.

The issue is that the complaint was presented in such a way that the possibility for communication was obliterated. A harsh start-up like *"I shouldn't have relied on you tonight. You never help out around here . . . ."* doesn't lead to dialogue—it leads to a dead end.

It's not the fact that a couple fights but *how* a couple fights that matters. In fact, couples who boast that they never disagree may face another issue, since resentments are likely to build up if issues are never addressed. No marriage is without its issues and disagreements, and avoidance of problems only causes issues to grow in significance and manifest in other ways. Never disagreeing with your husband may be a signal that feelings are not being expressed and that communication has broken down. So don't worry about fighting, but pay attention to fighting fairly.

How aware are you of the words you use in your home? How often do you tell someone to shut up or interrupt or raise the volume so you can be heard? Would you talk to your friends the way you talk to your spouse?

Of course, complaints are normal in any relationship, but there is a difference between a complaint and an attack. A couple who is highly critical of each other and who makes character assassinations is less likely to sustain healthy communication and connection over the long haul. With enough negative language, criticism, and harsh openings, Dr. Gottman warns, a couple can end up with contempt (sarcasm and name-calling), stonewalling (tuning someone out), and defensiveness (responding to every jab and feeling misunderstood). This pattern is lethal for two people, because all communication breaks down with this formula. Once this happens, the couple has a high likelihood for divorce.

If you constantly complain to your spouse that you are not fulfilled, or that your marriage or kids aren't fulfilling, the conversation is likely to head in a damaging direction. When you share such negative sentiments with your husband regularly, you may consider it benign venting, but your husband will internalize the issues you raise. If your husband perceives that what he is giving is not enough for you, his resulting sense of vulnerability may prompt him to shut down and disconnect or to become defensive and resentful.

Rather than speaking in terms of what you are missing, consider talking about what you want to have in your relationship and your life again, and what you hope to create with him together in partnership. If you feel the blahs in your marriage, enlist your partner to help you get back on track. Allow him to see that he's not the problem; rather, he is part of the solution.

PEOPLE WANT TO BE CHALLENGED, NOT CHANGED

One thing your husband undoubtedly fell for when dating you was the way you challenged him. Ideally, you still challenge him today.

Some women have lost confidence in who they are and have become "yes women" as a result, acquiescing to everything their husbands want instead of asserting their own wants. If this statement resonates with you, it is essential to modify your people-pleasing behavior and commit to articulating your position on a regular basis. Otherwise, you may become resentful and taken for granted in your marriage, and you will eventually disconnect from yourself. It doesn't feel good to ignore your instinct or to bury your needs. It doesn't serve you or your marriage. One of the reasons your husband wanted to be with you was because he appreciated that your perspective wasn't always the same as his own, that you expressed yourself.

Being a doormat in marriage is one thing; but there are women on the other side of the spectrum who are in the habit of telling their husbands what to do every day. We all need to recognize the difference between challenging someone and trying to change him. You married your man because you loved certain qualities in him. Even though many women joke about taking on a "project" and molding their man to their tastes, few men want us to tell them how to act. We're not their mothers; we are their wives, after all.

When you challenge your husband, ask yourself: Are you respecting his point of view and his values, or are you trying to make your husband more like yourself or to mold him into the idea of a good husband that your mother has? Nonstop nagging is a major issue in marriage, and one that causes more harm than we may realize. Continually telling your husband how he screwed up or why you are disappointed will result in your man feeling alienated, frustrated, and resentful. Besides, do you like yourself when you are a nag? You can challenge your husband without undermining his position.

DO YOU FIGHT TO WIN OR TO UNDERSTAND?

Many people enter a marital spat with boxing gloves on, prepared to knock down every point with a counterargument or an insult, creating a power struggle from the start. Rather than diffusing an argument by understanding or acknowledging the spouses' position, these people stay laser focused on their side of the story, anticipating what they'll say next (which means they're not listening to their spouses' position). They won't accept defeat, as if arguments between married couples are meant to create losers.

You may be quick on your feet when you get into a debate with a friend and always excel in closing deals at work, but marriage isn't an arena for competition. In marriage, we are on the same team as our spouses—so it makes little sense to have a clear winner and a loser in an argument. And if you're constantly setting up your spouse to lose each time you fight, you are helping to create a loser. Do you really want to be married to a loser?

One client I work with explained that when she argues with her husband, her blood pressure instantly rises and all logic flies out the window. This may be true, but it doesn't justify perpetuating a problem or making it worse.

You won't be heard more if you speak louder. Just because an argument brings out your emotions doesn't mean rules can be ignored. Sometimes, you have to count backward from three to one or take a time out to check in with yourself and make sure you are communicating effectively.

Three common techniques for arguing more effectively include looping, reframing, and speaking in terms of "I" versus "you."

Looping

Cara Raich, who works as a mediator with couples whose goal is to stay married, suggests that when couples initiate a cycle of attack and defend, they enter a conflict trap that is hard to get out of and as a result breeds resentment. In her practice, she models a popular communication technique called "looping" that helps couples communicate more effectively.

The point of looping is not to ensure that both spouses land on the same page; rather, it is to ensure that both parties hear one another's point of view. Here is an example of how a couple can communicate effectively by looping:

Wife: *I feel frustrated when you don't call to tell me you will be late from work, because then our dinner schedule gets off track. When dinner is pushed back, the kids take baths later and their bedtime is really late. I'm concerned that we will get into a bad habit as a family if we don't keep our schedules structured.*

Husband: *You are worried that eating schedules will affect bath and sleeping schedules and will get the family in trouble if they are not managed. For that reason, you want me to check in and tell you when I'll be late so you can plan better and we can stay on schedule as a family. Did I get that right?*

Wife: *Yes. Thanks.*

With this technique, the aim is not to repeat verbatim what your spouse expressed; the goal is for your spouse to know that you genuinely heard and acknowledged the concerns. The looping exercise forces your brain to listen and keep the attention on the person speaking so that you don't become distracted by formulating your counterattack. Once you close the loop by acknowledging that your partner captured your frustration accurately, dialogue and negotiation are more likely to take place.

The point of this exercise is not only for your spouse to hear your perspective, but for you to hear your position, too. When you hear your complaint spoken back to you, you may understand it better or tweak it so it more accurately reflects your feeling.

At first, the looping exercise may feel awkward or silly, but with practice, both husbands and wives start to shift the way they listen to each other and understand their own point of view.

Reframing

There's a saying that every argument has three sides—yours, the other person's, and the truth.

When we're in the heat of an argument, it can be difficult to see our own position from a different vantage point, but this is exactly the technique that will make us communicate more effectively. Reframing is a communication strategy that encourages the subject to put a new frame around his or her position, or someone else's position, so the picture looks different.

Considering the context in which something takes place or the intentions behind someone's actions helps people reframe a situation. Sometimes we get so hyperfocused on our own point of view that we can't see someone else's perspective clearly. We think about how an issue affects us and may forget that other people are affected as well. An important part of healthy communication includes compassion—seeing how things affect others and stepping away from our own perspective so that we can consider their experience.

I modeled the reframing technique recently with my friend Joe, who was annoyed that his wife, Natalie, never feels like making plans with his friends. I asked him to put himself in her shoes and defend her position. When Joe considered his wife's perspective, he realized that the issue is not that she doesn't like his friends; rather, she wants her husband to give her more advance notice so she can plan accordingly. She is a planner type and does not appreciate the spontaneity that he springs on her when his friends feel like heading out for a drink. Natalie has expressed that fact on numerous occasions, but Joe hardly heard it before recounting the scenario to me and looking at the situation from her vantage point. After seeing the issue through his wife's frame, he decided to tweak his approach; he believes it may produce a better result.

But the onus is not just on one person in a relationship to practice reframing. In this case, it would also be helpful for Natalie to consider her husband's perspective before expressing her disappointment when he spends time with his friends. It may be true that Natalie is more of a type A than Joe, but she married a spontaneous and social man (whom I used to jokingly refer to as a "type J"). She not only knew about Joe's social appetite, but she appreciated that about him. Natalie should support and nurture her husband's interests and respect that they don't always have to be her own. In fact, having different outlets and interests can serve her marriage, as we have discovered.

"I" versus "You"

A simple communication strategy, speaking in "I" versus "you," can lead to a more productive discussion. Shifting your language and speaking in the first person to express how you're feeling make you more likely to be heard. It's logical, really. Which statement would you respond better to? *You don't romance me anymore. It's as if you don't care.* OR *I loved when you used to take me on surprise dates. I miss that.*

WHAT'S YOUR INTENTION?

The underlying agreement that all couples should have, according to Cara Raich, is good intention. In other words, if you each acknowledge that you respect your spouse and your intent is not to hurt him or her, you're less likely to blame one another for hurt feelings. The next time you're upset with your husband, take a moment and ask yourself if you believe that he meant to hurt you with his words or actions. Consider that his intentions were probably not to cause harm.

Like anything that brings about positive change, demonstrating healthy communication patterns and putting yourself in another person's position takes conscious action, dedication, and practice.

What's the communication style of you and your spouse? Does one of you tend to be more confrontational or avoidant than the other?

If you're like most married couples, you and your spouse are environmentally friendly when it comes to your arguments: You recycle the same themes and complaints and have the same fight . . . often.

I asked several couples the question "What's your most popular argument with your spouse?" Each of the husbands and wives cited the same sources of conflict that their partners mentioned. Newlyweds Wendy and John have different opinions on what it means to keep the house nice. John thinks a nice home is a comfortable one, where he can relax; Wendy can't relax unless things in her home are in order. Wendy says that John doesn't always clean up after himself, and she gets irritated when he leaves things lying around or forgets to do simple domestic tasks, like making their bed after he wakes up. Wendy is the breadwinner in their relationship, and since John works from home on a few freelance projects, she expects that he will take care of their space when she is at the office.

John calls Wendy a "neat freak" and complains that she obsesses about things that are unimportant. When she gets stressed, he usually responds by telling her to relax (which, of course, puts Wendy more on edge!).

Little nuisances, like how clean you each keep your shared living space, are not unusual. In many cases, one partner has a more particular way to organize the home. Somehow, though, John and Wendy have managed to continue bickering over this issue since they moved in together 2 years ago. What John sees as anal-retentive and silly, Wendy sees as something that is important to her. Her husband's lack of attention to keeping the home as orderly as she'd like may be viewed as a sign of disrespect, since organization is one of her values. And stepping on someone's value is the easiest way to create tension.

Neither side is necessarily wrong in this case, but both have to see the other's point of view and consider where they can meet in the middle.

WHAT ATTRACTS YOU REPELS YOU

I often say that there is a fine line between endearing and annoying. I once heard former TV host Meredith Vieira say that her husband's humming used to be cute, and now it gets under her skin.

The qualities that may have initially attracted you to your husband when you were dating may be the very things you complain about now. Take my mom, a former English teacher, who used to find my dad's Hungarian accent cute and charming. Now she cringes when he pronounces a word incorrectly or gets his pronouns confused.

RECYCLING YOUR ARGUMENTS

Many couples recycle pain from the past when arguing. If you are in a pattern in which you repeatedly bring up an issue, like the time he lied to you about his whereabouts many years ago or how hurt you felt when he spoke to your mother with disrespect, it is important to isolate the argument and deal with it in therapy or by taking another approach. Arguing about an issue that happened in the past puts both of you in a difficult position, since you can't go back in time to fix it. The issue must be tackled with open communication and an agreement to work your way through it together so that you can find closure.

I spoke with Dori and Seth, who have been together for almost a decade, about what initially attracted them to each other. Dori cited Seth's sensitivity and laid-back nature. Seth was drawn to the way Dori was self-assured and direct. They felt comfortable around each other, and they balanced each other well.

Ten minutes later, I asked each of them what irks them most about their spouse. Dori talked about Seth's lack of attention to detail, and Seth said that his wife is so direct that sometimes it hurt his feelings. He wishes she would be more sensitive to his feelings.

Dori said, "He likes that I know what I want—except when it's directed at him." The root of this couple's most common argument stems from Dori's demanding approach and Seth's sensitive response—the exact qualities that drew them to each other in the first place.

If you loved that your partner was an energetic extrovert, you may later complain that he doesn't listen to you or let you get a word in edgewise. Or if you once admired your husband for being studious and well read, you may later find his observations pretentious.

It is important to recognize this theme, if it is one that resonates, so you can remember that the very quality you are now complaining about is the one that you once admired. Remind yourself why there is a good or charming side to the quality that now annoys you. Remember why the quality attracted you to your spouse in the first place.

Also consider that each good quality has a flip side that may be less appealing. For instance, when you fell for your husband, you may have loved how spontaneous and exciting he was; now you complain that he never makes plans in advance. If you loved that he was driven and successful, you must consider the other side to that driven quality when you complain that he works late. You can't have only the good side of his key characteristics, even though the positive aspects of his traits were the very things that stood out to you when you were dating him!

Is one of your biggest complaints about your husband something that you used to admire or appreciate about him?

APOLOGY ACCEPTED

Sometimes you want to focus on how your husband can handle something better, but other times in marriage it is important to focus on how *you* could have approached a situation more productively or thoughtfully.

When was the last time you told your husband that you were sorry for something you said or did (or didn't do) and meant it? Apologizing for speaking with disrespect to someone you love or for being inconsiderate of your husband's feelings is different from apologizing when you ask for what you need or want in a particular situation. (We know from Chapter 3 that those kinds of apologies lead to feelings of frustration and resentment.) So many of us view an apology, the kind of "sorry" we say when we take ownership of our mistakes, as an admission of defeat instead of as a gesture of reconciliation.

I interviewed a woman who has been married for 23 years, and she mentioned that she rarely apologizes to her spouse because she feels that once she tells him that she's sorry, all of her feelings will be discounted. "If I say I'm sorry, he won't understand that his actions bothered me," she explained.

The irony of apologizing (and meaning it) is that your position is more likely to be heard or accepted by the person you are saying sorry to (as long as your action didn't cause extreme pain or demonstrate significant disloyalty). I know I'm more receptive when someone expresses remorse and explains why he or she reacted a particular way. It gives me a better, and more full picture, of the situation.

The key to apologizing effectively is saying you are sorry in a way that is not only sincere but that keeps the focus on the person you hurt. If you add a "but" in your apology (i.e., "I'm sorry I did that, but I didn't know you would care . . ."), the recipient of your "sorry" may not find closure. In fact, he or she may grow more annoyed, because you are essentially dismissing why the action upset him or her in the first place. Genuinely taking ownership of your part in the misunderstanding or issue will result in the person you are apologizing to feeling acknowledged, making you both more likely to reach resolution.

There is something really mature and wonderful about owning your part of an argument when you offer a heartfelt "sorry." Give yourself an extra personal-growth point when you move from a framework of winning to one of understanding—and when you apologize for a situation you know you could have handled better.

FIVE TO ONE

When you and your future husband were dating and getting to know each other, chances are you used to have long conversations in which you listened intently to one another. You were genuinely curious about one another's interests and values. You wanted to make a good impression, so you likely gave him the benefit of the doubt when he said something you didn't agree with, and when you challenged him, you were careful with your words and didn't rush to judgment. Both of you probably took great care to make the small things matter, and you let the other know how much you cared on a daily basis.

In his studies on married couples, Dr. John Gottman determined that the essential ratio of positive to negative emotion displayed in an exchange is at least five to one. So for every time you put your partner down, it will take five times of acknowledging him, complimenting him, or showing him a kind gesture to achieve an overall happy state.

I know if I get a negative review or hear an insult, I remember it (or more accurately, obsess about it) much more than the positive reviews I read or compliments I receive. It's human nature.

How often do you tell your husband that you are proud of him or that he makes you happy? Do you acknowledge, in words, what he means to you? This may not come naturally, but the positive effects will make the effort worthwhile.

MEN AREN'T MIND READERS

You don't need me to tell you that, but it's a good reminder for many of us. I've been guilty of sulking and dragging around the house, hoping Michael would notice. When he does and says, "What's wrong?" I shrug, playing a silly game of "guess my gripe." But in these situations, Michael doesn't want hints. He wants answers. He wants direction. My husband can handle the truth!

If you're upset about something significant, it's up to you to communicate that. It's fine if you need a little time to collect your thoughts and don't want to talk right away. But take those steps to communicate so your husband doesn't feel cut off from what you're going through.

The formula for successful communication may sound like a lot of work, but it is actually quite simple: If you operate from the principle that you and your husband are on the same team, and that your ultimate goal is to keep that team together, you'll be more careful about the arguments you have and the way you have them. Your words do matter, so choose thoughtfully.

WIVES' TALE

The Boss

NAME: Mary
AGE: 43 years old
MARRIED: 15 years
CHILDREN: 11 and 13 years old

Scenario

Mary needs to put her signature on everything she touches. She feels that nobody can do anything as well as she can, and she believes she must direct most situations. She likes being seen as dominant and is quick to dismiss others' perspectives if she does not agree with them. She does not like weakness in herself or others, and she lives by the motto "Deal with it."

She challenges everyone in her family so much that her kids often avoid her, and her husband, Bill, is afraid to do anything around the house since he knows he will likely be criticized by his wife. He has started to check out, and Mary resents it.

Mary is a manager at her job and has a hard time switching off her work persona when she gets home. She sees her role in the family as the boss. She's incredibly protective and caring of her family and would do anything for them, but she is also extremely demanding and challenging.

Issue

Mary runs the risk of alienating everyone in her family, since she is critical of most things they do. She didn't marry her husband to be his mother, but she often treats him like her third child. (Her husband may enable this behavior by rebelling against Mary's bullying or being defensive and childlike in his response.) Bill ignores his wife's rants and hardly pitches in at home because he hates being corrected every minute.

Mary does not see how her intimidation and constant demands for respect cause people to avoid her. Regular nagging means that Mary's family will eventually tune her out completely, as they have already started to do. The cycle easily breaks down healthy communication—and once that is disrupted, a healthy family dynamic is broken.

Solution

Mary must learn that her nonstop demands and excessive control over everybody and everything will make her feel *less* in control. Even if her intentions are good when she assumes the role of boss, she must recognize the difference between providing for her family and being overly dominant with them.

Take a Step Back

When the instinct to nag her husband and fix his behavior comes up, Mary should take a deep breath, *before* being reactive, and remind herself that her husband is an adult who is capable of making decisions. He's out in the world every day without her influencing his actions. She should think about what she was going to say and replace it with something that will be more likely to be heard by her husband. She can adopt the motto "should say" so that she can keep their communication healthy. For instance, if Mary was going to say, "You put the dishes away in the wrong places!" she can pause and consider her "should say." After a moment, she might edit the feedback to "Thank you for putting the dishes away." (In some cases, she might decide to say nothing at all.)

Channel Energy Elsewhere

Since Mary feels aggression and stress, she may want to channel her energy through a more productive activity, like kickboxing.

Mary may also want to imagine what it would be like to be in her husband's shoes. How would it feel if he were constantly correcting her behavior and picking on everything she did or did not do? Would she like to be controlled?

CHAPTER FIVE

Take a Time Out: Cheat On Your Kids

My friend Beth told me about the hot date night she and her husband, Mark, planned last year. They were heading to the nicest lookout in the city on a warm Saturday night, something they hadn't done since they met 7 years earlier. She put on her sexiest lingerie, doused herself in the perfume she knew Mark loved, and had compiled a list of cute cafés they could visit after the sunset. She was planning to start kissing Mark in the car on the way home, just like she used to when they were dating. She knew it would drive him crazy, and she was excited for the outcome. She and Mark had not gone out on a date in ages. With her hair wet and the menu of a charming café open on her computer, the phone rang. Her sister had a migraine and would not be able to babysit Beth and Mark's daughter after all. Beth and Mark wouldn't have a date night for another 6 months.

I asked my friend why she waited so long to reschedule an evening out. She was clearly excited about the night, and her husband was, too. She sighed, "It's hard to plan a date when I barely have time to do anything. Honestly, I didn't feel like exerting all the energy again."

Unless you were a single parent when you were dating your future spouse, babysitting and feeding schedules didn't get in the way of a fun night out. A movie date didn't cost you close to a hundred dollars because of ticket prices and the babysitter's fee, and you were able to keep your eyes open for the entire film because you weren't exhausted from parental duties.

A number of parents I interviewed felt that they were not spending enough time with their children; however, a recent study conducted at the University of California, San Diego, showed that parents spend more time with their kids now than they did a decade ago. This time together is not always in the home; many parents spend significant hours each week driving their children to after-school activities and cheering them on at soccer games and dance recitals. Tara Parker-Pope referenced the study in the 2010 *New York Times* article "Surprisingly, Family Time Has Grown." As Parker-Pope wrote, "Before 1995, mothers spent an average of about 12 hours a week attending to the needs of their children. By 2007, that number had risen to 21.2 hours a week for college-educated women." Add to increased parenting duties and expectations the fact that most workers face increased hours in this economic climate, plus all of the time spent on household chores, and it's no wonder that most mothers I spoke with would rather take a nap than have a night out on the town.

When you're a mother, it is difficult and maybe less appealing to date your husband—but it's even more important. Studies consistently show that on average, married couples are more satisfied in their lives than singles until children enter the picture. Harvard psychologist Dr. Daniel Gilbert, who has written extensively about happiness, examined the effects of children on marital happiness. He has written that he's never seen a study that showed a positive correlation between children and happiness in marriage. Dr. Gilbert acknowledges that children can be a couple's greatest blessing, but on a day-to-day level, they can also be the source of tremendous stress in a relationship. Once kids enter a marriage, couples are more likely to stay together but are also more likely to report dissatisfaction.

Of course, few parents would say that their kids are a source of their discontent in their marriage. Quite the contrary—most would cite their children as their greatest accomplishment and deepest joy. I don't know anybody who regrets the choice to have children, but many of these same people recognize that romance, intimacy, and positive communication have broken down in their relationships since they became parents. Few realize how detrimental this is to their marriages until it becomes painfully apparent, sometimes after years of resentments have built up.

Couples who have children and don't consider themselves to be happily married often say they're simply too tired and under too much stress to enjoy life. They say that they can hardly remember what life was like (with or without their spouses) before they were parents. Herein lies the problem: When you embrace the role of

MOMMY BLOGGERS

The popularity of "mommy blogs" underscores the need for connection and support among mothers today. In 2008, journalist Katie Couric reported that there were 36 million female bloggers and women interacting with female blogs, a number of which were mommy blogs, and that number had increased each year. Blogs written by and for mothers are some of the fastest-growing niche sites in the blogosphere (BlogHer is one example), and conferences like the Mom 2.0 Summit give women a change to discuss varied issues. I asked a frequent visitor to mommy blogs why she's interested in the sites, and she responded, "I need to know my experience is normal. It helps to share with other mothers. It saved me in my first year of motherhood!"

being a parent in addition to being a spouse, it's easy to lose some of yourself in the process. And when you lose your own identity, it's hard to feel happy in your marriage or in your life.

What do you miss most about your marriage pre-parenthood?

PAY ATTENTION

Michael and I have five plants in our home. A few look so pathetic and malnourished that I avoid looking at them when I walk by. The ficus that sits in our front window, however, looks radiant. It's our prized plant—prettier than the day we took it home from the store. (I feel like a fraud, as people passing by the window would think I have a green thumb.) Not surprisingly, this plant gets the most sunlight, water, and attention. The fern sitting on my desk, on the other hand, is drooped over. Each day, I have to pick its shriveled leaves off my keyboard.

It occurred to us recently that we shouldn't play favorites with our plant family. So over the past few weeks, we've given each plant a chance to spend some time in the prized window position. A few of them are starting to perk up, while some continue their decline.

If your kids are getting all the sunlight in your life, chances are you and your husband don't have much warmth left for one another. All of us need proper care and nourishment to thrive. Sometimes you and your spouse have to give one another that prized window seat and turn the focus back to each other, yourselves, and your marriage. Your kids may be your pride and joy, but they are not the only ones who need your attention.

How can you find time to reconnect with your husband when you barely have time to take a shower? The reality is that you have to make time for your marriage, just as you would with anything that is a priority in your life.

Sari and Matt, who have been married for almost a dozen years and juggle demanding jobs and responsibilities to their two young boys, don't recognize themselves in the statistics of married couples who have lost their romantic connection since having children. In many ways, they say, their connection has deepened because they have a powerful, shared purpose as parents.

After becoming parents, they set a goal to continue date nights at least once a month and to take vacations without the kids until their children were old enough to remember and appreciate such trips. The precedent was set when their first-born was only 3½ months old. Sari and Matt traveled from the West Coast to attend a friend's wedding in Vermont. They left their baby son with their parents and felt guilty about it . . . until they didn't. They quickly realized that getting away together was just what their relationship needed. When they booked the weekend trip to Vermont, they had been living like co-workers, taking parental shifts, and running on empty. The wedding getaway was helpful for each of them individually and good for them as a couple.

"Going to that wedding together was a turning point for us in our marriage," Matt recalled. "We thought people would scream at us for leaving our baby at home, but not one person did. In fact, most said 'I get it.' We knew, moving forward, that

KIDS LIKE DATE NIGHT

Even though your kids don't join you on a date, you can still involve them in the planning and get them excited about it. Ask your children to help you pick the date spot or choose what you should wear. The more they are involved, the more understanding they will be when you and your husband head out for your special date night.

we had to dedicate time together away from our duties as parents. It became a priority."

Sari and her husband happily spend most of their free time with their kids, but they have managed to find windows dedicated to their own separate interests and to outings together. Recently, their oldest asked his dad with a smile, "Do you and Mommy kiss before or after your date?" Before Matt could answer, his son added, "I think you should kiss for the whole date!" There is no question that kids enjoy the fact that their parents love each other and find ways to express it.

15 MINUTES A DAY

A survey of 4,500 parents commissioned in 2008 by Holiday Inn found that couples in the United Kingdom spend, on average, 15 minutes a day having a real conversation (5 minutes in the morning and 10 minutes in bed). Most of the time, when married parents communicate, they do so in order to coordinate plans, talk about the kids' needs, or voice concerns. Sound familiar?

I asked a dozen couples with children to log how long their uninterrupted conversations lasted in a given day, and most came in around 18 minutes or less. In contrast, when they were dating each other, they often spent hours talking with their partners. One couple described their current practice: "We check in briefly when one of us is in the car—that seems to be the best time. It's hard to not multitask, even with your communication, when your day is packed and your children demand your attention."

Relationships break down when communication dissolves. If lack of "talk time" with your spouse is a problem that resonates with you, it is essential to rebuild this aspect of your marriage before the lack of regular (adult) communication affects your connection. It's not just the quantity of time spent communicating with your partner, but the quality of your conversations that you need to be aware of, as we discovered in Chapter 4.

Consider what you may have to say no to in your schedule to say yes to more time and connection with your spouse. What's one step you can take this month to get closer to your goal?

YourTango.com addressed the need for marriage talk time in a recent online article by Lori Lowe. Lowe wrote, "My husband and I have recently begun taking 15 minutes after dinner to talk together in our sunroom. We ask the children to play or read on their own for that short amount of time. (The youngest is still learning not to interrupt us. The oldest finds it helpful to set a timer.) Find a time in your day that works for you. It's amazing how a short time each day can help you feel reconnected."

One of the couples who responded to my question spends approximately 20 to 30 minutes talking and connecting almost every day, which has helped strengthen their marriage. The wife remarked, "The kids are in bed by 8:00, and we take a moment to clean up; but before we flip on the television in separate rooms and our eyes glaze over (or before my husband falls asleep in front of the TV), we make a point to catch up on the day and reconnect. Everything else can wait. If we are too tired to talk, we spend a few minutes sharing physical affection . . . anything to foster closeness. If we didn't make a decision to do this together, it probably would never happen."

These women are on to something—talk time won't just *happen*. Whenever you start a conversation, you may have a toddler tugging at your leg or one of a dozen things to get through on your day's checklist. You have to consider building the time—perhaps only a focused 10 or 15 minutes—into your day and make it a daily priority. Use your 15 minutes to catch up and connect, just as you would if you were dating. Set a rule not to spend your designated talk time discussing the kids, your finances, or housework. Notice how differently you and your husband connect once you take the time to talk every day—and how that refreshed connection affects your marriage.

THE BIRDS AND THE BEES

Experts generally agree that babies under the age of 6 months can be exposed to their parents having (loving) sex without being affected; however, the older your child gets, the more you have to figure out creative ways to keep junior outside the bedroom.

Matt and Sari find that since becoming parents, they have less energy at bedtime than they used to, so now they opt for what they call the "afternoon delight" while their children are napping. Other couples, like Genevieve and her husband, Mike, have had to tweak their sex schedule from morning to evening now that their kids don't nap (and love to jump into bed with them as soon as they wake up!).

Once your little ones are no longer taking naps but still climb into bed with you after a scary dream at night, you may have to think of another time—or place—for sex. If your child constantly swings open your bedroom door at unexpected times, consider having a secret rendezvous in another area of the house, like the guest bedroom or the bathroom, where you can close the door and keep the baby monitor on. You could also simply choose to lock your bedroom door or instate a "no entering without knocking" rule. It's healthy for your kids to understand that you and your husband are entitled to private time. If they really need you or want your attention, this may not prevent them from trying to get in the room, but at least it will give you an opportunity to regroup before they charge in.

If your child catches you in the act, he or she may not understand what you are doing and might have many questions. I'll never forget the story of my cousin, then 5 years old, making his way between his naked parents in bed. They were having sex and didn't realize their son was in the room (in the bed!) with them until he tapped his dad to ask, "Why are you doing that to Mommy?" His mother's first response was, "Daddy and I do this because we love each other." To which the 5-year-old replied, "I love you, too. I want to play!" Yikes.

If your child catches you midromp, put your clothes back on and take your child back to his or her room. You may have to comfort your daughter or son, since sex can be confusing or even scary to a child. Explain that you and Daddy were having private time, and that everything is all right. Put the attention back on your child, and pick up sex with your spouse another time.

In general, we should expose our children to loving acts, like kissing and cuddling with our partners, but not to sex. You don't want to be forced to have the birds and the bees talk before you believe your child is ready for it.

CHEAT ON YOUR KIDS

I don't know if you've noticed, but there seems to be a trend for parents to take their kids everywhere—concerts, nice restaurants, theatre, gallery openings. While it's wonderful to expose your children to the world around them, sometimes it's also necessary to enjoy adults-only time.

I was at a bustling French restaurant in Brooklyn recently. At 9:00 p.m., I thought I was imagining the sound of children's whimpers nearby. Then I noticed two little boys trying to build something with their cutlery. Both kids appeared to be bored, tired, and cranky. The parents seemed a little tired and cranky as well. One of my friends commented that she feels guilty each time she leaves her three-year-old with a babysitter and understands why some parents never want to leave their kids behind for anything.

Do you feel like you are cheating your kids when you take a time out away from them?

When I was growing up, my parents took me and my sister on fun trips and out to great restaurants, but they also left us with a sitter on many Saturday nights. I'm sure I moaned, whined, cried, and stomped my feet for the first few minutes when they left for their date, but I also remember being excited to have a fun teenage babysitter hang out with us.

Children are amazingly adaptable. As you get accustomed to having a special scheduled night with your spouse, date night will also become normal to your kids. They will understand that a night out is part of their parents' lives. In fact, when you show your children that you are making your marriage a priority and taking time just for you and your husband, you are modeling good relationship behavior. Children like to see their parents getting along. They may cringe when you're affectionate in front of them, but they'd certainly rather witness a hug and a kiss than a fight.

I've heard parents lament that the cost of childcare prohibits them from taking time for themselves. These days, reliable baby-sitters and nannies can charge a small fortune. After paying for childcare, you may not have a lot of money left over for your date with your husband—but don't use that as an excuse to skip scheduling time alone together. Some of the best dates in life are free! In my research with singles, interesting experiences always score higher than fancy meals at expensive restaurants in terms of overall date satisfaction. Novel experiences—activities you try together for the first time—also trigger the pleasure centers of our brain and therefore help us register our connection with our date (even if it is our husband) as new and fresh.

Top Five Cheap Date Ideas

Adventure Date: Tourist in the City

Ever notice that you haven't visited some of the top tourist sites of your city in a while—or ever? Is there a fabulous lookout with a panoramic view or a famous landmark that you learned about in school? Is there a cute neighborhood you haven't explored? Have you taken all of the scenic walking trails or tours that visitors typically access?

Write down some of the spots in your area that you've heard or read about but haven't seen, and then let your creative juices flow. Book a date to go to one of the locations, and bring a camera to capture the date (just as you would on vacation!). Discovering new areas and landmarks with your spouse will create new memories and remind you how much is left to discover together.

Exotic Date: Ethnic Cuisine

Check online reviews and find a Thai, Vietnamese, Chinese, or Indian restaurant in your area with good ambience. Ethnic restaurants tend to be cheaper than your usual white-tablecloth bistros and may add spice to your routine. Sample exotic dishes together and stimulate your taste buds.

Active Date: Play Together

Sharing a physical activity will boost endorphins and may also bring out a fun, competitive, flirting spirit. Play Frisbee, go jogging, or take a hike. Challenging your body and sharing a common goal with your spouse (like completing a hiking trail) will reinforce your bond. If you are playing a competitive sport, like tennis, make sexy bets to amp up the flirtation.

Cultural Date: Experience Live Music or a Museum

Whether you reside in a big city or a small town, there are always talented musicians performing for a low cover price to build their fan base. Check out your local music listings to find the style of music that you enjoy most and head out to support a local musician—often for under $10.

Head to the museum for a special talk or take advantage of the "pay what you can" discounts offered by many institutions.

RESOURCES

If you don't have trusted family members in the area to watch your children, it can be difficult to figure out how to schedule a day or night date without your kids. Your local community center, church, synagogue, or mosque may have some excellent resources. You may also consider checking out well-rated babysitting Web sites (complete with references) like Sittercity.com and GoNannies.com.

You may decide to explore local galleries, which are usually free to enter, to see the work of featured artists.

Sexy Date: Book a Hotel

I used to work with someone who would take her husband to cheap motels for date nights. "The seedier the better!" she told me. There was something about being in a totally new environment, without worrying that the kids would walk in or thinking about the laundry yet to be done, that put her and her husband in the mood. Enjoying time together in a hotel in your city will make your date a memorable one (even if you just decide to stay in and order breakfast in bed with a pay-per-view movie).

Note: If you can't spare a night away, consider finding a day rate for an afternoon rendezvous! Many motels and hotels have cheap midweek specials that you can find on a discount hotel Web site.

Five Things That Do Not Count as a Date

- Watching television together

- Taking a trip to Home Depot, Costco, or the grocery store

- Going to the local restaurant that you take your kids to (and that is full of children)

○ Enjoying a great date spot . . . with your kids

○ Talking about the kids (or finances) for the duration of the date

DATE NIGHT IN

"It all seems like too big of a production," one of my clients admitted when she told me why she and her spouse don't make a habit of romancing each other.

If you've never left your kids at home while you and your husband went out, scheduling a full-fledged date can feel like a daunting and challenging prospect. And if you have a newborn at home, it's unrealistic to simply pick up and head out for a night on the town. In these cases, make baby steps toward renewing your connection with your husband rather than avoiding romance altogether.

My cousin Sharon, who has an 8-month-old girl, attended her brother-in-law's wedding with her daughter when her baby was just a couple of months old. Sharon was sleep deprived and low on energy, but she still wanted to enjoy the wedding with her husband and dance with him. Instead, she sat in the corner with her baby, totally exhausted, and watched as everyone else had fun.

If she had to do it again, she told me, she would bring a babysitter with her so she could step away and join the celebration with her husband. "It would have been worth a little money to have help so I could enjoy the party and dance with my husband but still be near my baby," she said.

My friend Kara can relate to mothers who don't feel ready for date night out, but she can't relate to those who avoid romance with their spouses altogether. Kara works at a busy job, has a 1½-year-old son, and is expecting her second child, but she makes a habit of enjoying date nights in with her husband, David. She has not been interested in leaving her son with a babysitter, as she sees him for only a couple of hours a day during the workweek, so she and David make sure to schedule romantic time together at home. She said she schedules connection time with her husband to ensure it doesn't get overlooked in their hectic lives. When David and Kara have date night in, they agree not to make their son the focus of their attention.

"David and I find romantic time or together time by taking long walks when it's nice outside and doing things we enjoy, like cooking dinner or playing with our son without the TV on," Kara said. "It might sound silly, but during those times, though our son is still with us, he's not the focus of our attention, and we're connecting with one another. We try hard to sit down and have dinner together as a family, which helps us take time to reflect on our day and share . . . . It would be so easy to just talk about our son, or to keep busy and not slow down."

Monika and Dave have a regularly scheduled date night at home while their 3-year-old and 6-year-old are sleeping. They've started a tradition of choosing a new cuisine each month to learn to master together in the kitchen. Last month, they tried to perfect their Indian cooking skills.

According to Monika, "Once we put the kids to bed, we turn on nice music, dim the lights, and Dave starts chopping the vegetables while I clean up a few things around the house. We work on the recipe together and eat by candlelight. What we're experiencing is new and gives us an opportunity to connect."

After planning romantic time at home, as these couples have, you may decide to take the next step toward dating your husband. Your next move may be for you and your spouse to go away from home during the day, for lunch or a walk, while you leave your child with a trusted caregiver. After assessing your comfort level and getting used to leaving your baby for a short period of time, you may work your way up to a night on the town and, eventually, a night out of town.

Once you experience your first date night with your husband, you will likely get more comfortable making it a regularly scheduled event. As one woman I interviewed who insists on date nights out admitted, "I love being with my baby, but there's something really nice about going to a place where grown-ups go, putting on a beautiful outfit, and knowing slobber or snot won't end up on it!" (Her comment reminded me of another mother I met, who mentioned that her husband used to drool all over her on dates, and now it's only her baby who drools on her.)

The most important thing is to plan dates that feel natural and fun to you—don't worry about anybody's guidelines for what you should do. Think about the things you and your husband used to enjoy doing together before marriage—the things that make you feel connected, excited, and comfortable with each other.

But don't dismiss something you haven't tried for fear that it won't work. You may think that the idea of date night feels too contrived or that it adds too much pressure to your relationship,

THE KID SWAP

Kid swaps are another way couples with children find time to date. The idea behind the swap is to take turns with good friends and trusted members of your community who will watch the kids so the adults don't have to worry about a sitter. One Saturday night, you may have a playdate with your neighbor's children; the following week, that neighbor may take your kids. Assuming the children play well and are relatively well behaved, this can be a win-win for everyone.

but consider the big picture and how the erosion of the connection in your marriage will affect you over the long term. Besides, once you incorporate romantic connection and regular communication back into your relationship, you will realize how much you miss connecting as lovers—not just as parents.

ASK FOR HELP

In past generations, it was common for an extended family to live on the same block or in the same neighborhood and for everyone to participate in child rearing. Today, many of us live far from our families. We need to scope out and create our own network of support when we are parents, or we may feel lonely and overwhelmed.

On a recent flight back to New York from our anniversary trip to Jamaica, Michael and I met Marie, a bubbly stewardess who is a mother of four. Her kids are old enough now to take care of each other, but there was a period when she had four children under 10 years old and no family around to pitch in and help. Her church and community's support were invaluable at that time in her life as a mother. She advises other moms to surround themselves with friends and community members (especially when family isn't around), or parenthood will feel overwhelming. And without the help of others, it is certainly difficult to put attention on your primary relationship with your spouse.

Marie said, "My friends rallied around me when I needed help. I hit rock-bottom a few times and felt completely scared with the realities of raising four little ones. I realized that I always help others—and it was okay now for me to ask—it was my turn! My friends and community were wonderful. Women shouldn't be scared to ask for what they need."

Marie's advice is straightforward, but it's not that easy to follow for those of us who don't want to burden others. Sometimes we have to ask for support. If we try to be superwomen and do it all, we run the risk of losing ourselves or disconnecting from our marriages.

Don't wait to reconnect with your spouse until your children have graduated from high school or until problems in your marriage threaten to end it. Dating your husband is not mutually exclusive from being a parent. Sure, you may not crave intimacy when you're changing diapers, but when you see your husband reading a nighttime story to your little one, or helping your child with a school project, he may become even more irresistible to you.

When you have young children, dating your husband can be a challenge—but it should never be a burden. He's the partner you chose to marry because he enhances your life. Find time in your day and your week to remember that and to create the time and space for adult connection.

WIVES' TALE

Always Planning, Never Present

NAME: Judy
AGE: 36 years old
MARRIED: 8 years
CHILDREN: 4, 6, and 7 years old

Scenario

Judy has never felt the "7-year itch" in her marriage because she's barely had time to scratch herself. A year into her marriage, she and her husband, Paul, had their first child; their two other children followed shortly after. Life hasn't stopped since they became parents, and Judy and her husband feel like roommates, not lovers.

Judy's kids go to extracurricular classes all week—music, gymnastics, and swimming—and she often feels like a mother, chauffeur, camp director, and a short-order cook rolled up in one. She always seems to be rushing to her next post. All of her kids are in bed by 9:00, and after she cleans up, she conks out in front of the television, exhausted by 10:00. Her life is moving so rapidly that she often feels she is operating on mommy autopilot. When her alarm goes off early in the morning, the cycle starts all over again.

Issue

Judy can't be present as a woman, a wife, and a mother because she always feels she needs to think 10 steps ahead to make sure everyone's schedules are organized. Her husband, Paul, initiates sex, but her "honey, I'm tired" is hardly even an excuse. Lately, the two have been like ships passing in the night, only catching up periodically via text messages during the day. Paul complains that the more time that passes without intimacy, the more they get used to that situation—and the more they fight. He can't even stop Judy to have a conversation with her once the children are tucked in, because she has a long laundry list to get through before the end of the week. Judy has prioritized her tasks over her connection with her husband. He wants his wife to relax and to find a way to be more in the moment so she can enjoy her life. He knows that if she continues at this pace, their connection will only grow weaker.

Solution

Judy risks wearing herself out to the point that she won't be useful to anyone in her family. She needs to put some attention back on herself and learn to delegate some of her to-dos. If she arranged more carpools for the kids, hired a cleaning person to come in a few times a month, enlisted her husband's help, and/or put the kids to bed a little earlier, she might find a few more moments to breathe.

Reconnect with Passions

Judy should take an hour a week to indulge in one of her passions. For instance, if she started to work out again and to go jogging, an activity that helps her clear her head, her stress levels might dissipate and her energy would increase. Additionally, working out boosts energy levels and pumps endorphins.

Practice Presence

To achieve her desire to be present in her fast-paced environment, Judy may want to start each day 10 minutes earlier with a short meditation before the hustle and bustle in her house begins. Or she may end her day with a warm bath before she climbs into bed. She may also decide to build 10 to 15 minutes in for talk time with her spouse after the kids go to bed and/or commit to a once-a-month date night to get away from her hectic schedule.

If she feels that she does not have 10 minutes for meditation, Judy can start with 2 minutes of concentrated breathing in a private area of her home (even the bathroom would work!) so she can center herself before getting drawn into the day's activities.

PART TWO

STOP COMPLAINING AND START CREATING

One of the significant issues in marriage that we don't discuss enough is not money or sex, it's not child-rearing or in-law challenges, and it's not about the lack of time we have to connect with each other. A real problem in our marriages, one that many of us don't freely admit, is plain and simple BOREDOM.

Some people feel guilty admitting it, but most married couples agree that it's a challenge to sustain interest in their partner every day for years . . . and years. Who wants to hear her husband's rant again about how we can put a man on the moon but can't solve the issue of dropped calls? Or about the real estate investment he should've made years ago? Or whether the plumber is overcharging to fix the leak in the bathroom?

On a long drive this summer, Michael and I joked about not speaking too much the night before so we would have something to talk about on our car trip. I don't think we were kidding. I imagine that boredom is reciprocal in most relationships. Over the holidays with family recently, I watched as Michael mouthed the punchline as I was telling one of my favorite stories. I felt like we were reenacting a lame sitcom scene.

One of my friends admitted recently that she doesn't understand how she can be bored in her marriage when her life is busier than ever and she is pulled in all directions. "With my schedule, it's shocking that I can be bored at all," she said in disbelief. But it's easy to get bored in your marriage. There's a big difference between *doing* and *being*.

As a self-professed pleasure-seeker, I used to believe that my life with my husband should always be interesting. Not even just interesting, but stimulating! Exciting! Sometimes, though, it should just . . . be. Like anything in life, marriage has wonderful rewards, challenging events, and long uneventful periods. It's not realistic to always expect the passionate exchanges and crazy fireworks that were present when things with our partners were unknown and new. Occasional boredom isn't a signal that our relationships aren't working or that we didn't marry the right person. In fact, it may be a sign that things are perfectly normal.

You hear about the ups and downs in marriage but rarely hear about the simple reality: Keeping your relationship interesting and sexy over time isn't easy. Being with the same person for years can be wonderfully gratifying and, at times, terribly boring. I like to refer to this state of relationship ennui as the marriage "blahs."

I suggest taking a three-pronged approach to fighting the blahs.

I. PRACTICE ACCEPTANCE

Let me qualify this step with a disclaimer: Don't accept monotony in your marriage every day for years, or you will want to escape your relationship. Being complacent in a partnership generally reinforces the problem and magnifies it, but by practicing acceptance, you give yourself—and your husband—a gentle break on those days when you're just tired or overwhelmed by life's stressors and feel like temporarily checking out. Boredom can force you to slow down or stop—which may be just what you need.

Accept your state of boredom, without fighting it or feeling bad about it, and you may realize that there is peace and comfort in the quiet "boring" part of your marriage.

2. BE PRESENT

I took a moment the other day to bask in appreciation. I made a point to take inventory of all of the blessings in my life. I focused my attention on the amazing things my husband does for me and for our family. I looked around at our new home that we worked hard to buy. I admired the half-finished table that my husband is building and reflected on how much thought and care has gone into creating it. (Before focusing my positive attention on it, it just looked like an unfinished lump in the room that I was eager to move.) I closed my eyes and pictured Michael making a funny face and doing one of his hilarious impressions, and I started to laugh out loud.

When your marriage appears stale, dedicate a few moments to shift your attention to the beauty around you and in your life. Being present when we are "bored" reminds us that there are many blessings around us—we just need to take the time to acknowledge them.

3. TAKE ACTION

The other side of acceptance is action. You can choose to accept the moments of boredom in your marriage and surrender to them, *and* you can take active steps toward making your relationship more dynamic. Taking action is about putting verbs in your sentences, so you are not just complaining about the state of your union.

A friend of mine mentioned that she is in a perpetual state of numbness—disinterested in everything around her and indifferent to her husband's words and affection. Her marriage isn't yet in crisis mode, but she knows that if she continues to surrender to her marital blahs every day without finding some balance and joy, they're bound to travel down a shaky road.

In Part II, we will examine how to add a little more spice and excitement to your marriage so boredom can be something you experience occasionally, not constantly. In this section, we will also explore infidelity and examine not only why some people cheat but what you can do if you've become so bored that you've begun to fantasize about adding some excitement to your life with someone who's not your husband.

There's a popular saying, "The cure for boredom is curiosity. There is no cure for curiosity."

While sex is a significant part of "cheating with your husband," it is not the only way to increase intimacy, connection, and excitement. Simple tweaks and deliberate steps toward connection can create big changes (and a lot more fun!) in your marriage.

What actions are you willing to take to create the marriage you imagined on your wedding day? What steps will help breathe some new vitality into your relationship? Are you going to surrender to a life of the blahs—or are you up for the challenge?

CHAPTER SIX

Cheating On Your Husband

(with Someone Who's Not Your Husband)

Years ago, when I was spending time with a friend who was engaged, her mother shared stories with us about her own 30-year marriage. She described it as a happy union but admitted there'd been a few bumps along the way.

She told us about an event that occurred in her second year of marriage that would become a defining moment in her relationship with herself and with her husband. At the time, she worked as a nurse in a hospital with a young, handsome doctor who was charming and flirtatious. Before long, she looked forward to their daily flirty exchanges. She started to wake up earlier to apply her makeup and do her hair. She dreamed about this doctor when she went to bed, and he was the first image in her head when she woke up. She looked forward to work. Months into the crush, there was palpable sexual tension between them. It was clear that he had a crush on her as well, and he started to send her more overt signals. She knew that if she allowed it, something would happen.

As I was listening to this tale, part of me was rooting for her very wonderful and sweet husband, and another part of me was excited about the crush. I could barely wait for the next part of the story. "What happened?" we asked. What. Happened?!

She told us about the morning she walked into work confidently and with the same sass that made the doctor fall for her in the first place. She marched over to the administration office on the fourth floor and said, "I request to be placed on another floor, in a different department."

Not what we were expecting.

Life is about choices, and every day we make choices that not only affect us as individuals but also affect our spouses and the sanctity of our marriages.

At the boiling point of this woman's exchange with her crush, she made a conscious decision to remove herself from the situation. She knew that if she pursued something with the doctor, it would change her life forever. She didn't trust that the crush would subside or that she would stop daydreaming about him—she liked him and was attracted to him, and it was clear that he was attracted to her. Once she started to lose trust in herself, she decided to take control of the situation.

INCREASED ACCESS

These days, you can't open an entertainment magazine (or, sadly, a newspaper) without reading about a celebrity cheating scandal. Political figures, sports heroes, musicians, late-night talk show hosts, and movie stars apparently cheat on their spouses so frequently that the faithful and marriage-minded public figures would probably make for more shocking headlines.

With all the scandalous stories reported every day, it may appear that adultery is more common than ever before. In reality, it is hard to gather accurate data on the number of men and women who have cheated on their spouses now or in any era. Not surprisingly, a majority of those involved in extramarital affairs don't want to disclose the truth of their indiscretions for fear of being caught or judged, especially when a survey or study is conducted in person. (In one study of infidelity conducted by the University of Colorado and Texas A&M, 1 percent of women admitted to cheating on their husbands when they were interviewed in person, whereas 6 percent of women fessed up to infidelity when they submitted their answers anonymously via computer.)

While data on adultery are difficult to collect and quantify, we do see a connection today between factors in our modern lifestyle—including the ubiquitous presence of technology in our lives and longer hours spent working away from home—and extramarital relations. It's not fair to say that these factors *cause* cheating, but they certainly give us more access to romantic and sexual relationships outside the home.

Technology provides more avenues for infidelity than have ever been available to us. Typically, mobile phones, which offer the opportunity for discreet calls and texts, are one of the first devices suspicious spouses check when they have a hunch a spouse has strayed. And popular online social networks like Facebook that reunite old friends (and exes) offer the opportunity to develop new connections, rekindle old flames, and provide a fun, virtual escape for people in unfulfilling relationships at home. According to a study conducted by the Pew Research Center, 20 percent of adults who used social networking sites in 2008 admitted to "innocent" e-flirting. The trend is so prevalent that a pastor in New Jersey recently addressed his married congregants with the edict *Thou Shalt Not Facebook*. The pastor shared the advice after 20 couples among the 1,100 people who attend his church reported marital problems that they attributed to spouses reconnecting with past loves on the site.

Some online dating sites estimate that approximately one-third to a quarter of their users are in committed relationships.

When interviewed, married men and women who have used dating sites to find relationships outside their marriages admitted to initially perusing the sites out of curiosity before eventually logging in to look for and actively solicit dates. There are even online dating sites that encourage infidelity. AshleyMadison.com, whose motto is "Life is Short. Have an Affair," reports a membership of more than 7 million married people.

But while constant access to technology can aid and abet cheaters, it can just as easily expose them. I recently heard about a man who checked in on Foursquare (a location-based social media application), which tipped off his wife that he'd lied to her about his whereabouts. Never have there been so many opportunities to be tagged and discovered in real time.

MODERN CHEATING

The increased hours that American workers are spending at their jobs also offer more time and space for extramarital dalliances. According to the National Sleep Foundation, more than one-third of Americans report working 10 or more hours a day (Dolly Parton's anthem for the working girl, "Nine to Five," is apparently outdated). A survey conducted by Harris Interactive concluded that 72 percent of Americans check work e-mail outside their regular business hours. Even when we are away from the office, we are still connected.

Americans are also assigned fewer vacation days, take shorter lunches, and log more hours on the job than just a decade ago. Juliet Schor, author of the 1992 bestseller *The Overworked American*, reported that in 1990 Americans worked approximately 1 month more per year than they had in 1970. Nearly a decade after that, a Bureau of Labor Statistics report showed that in 1999, 20.5 percent of the American workforce reported to log at least 49 hours a week on the job, up significantly from a few years prior. And in 2007, less than a decade after that report was published, Tara Weiss, career columnist for *Forbes* magazine, wrote "How Extreme Is Your Job?" and asserted that the 70-hour workweek is becoming the norm in the American workplace. Weiss continues to share her perspective on staying competitive and employed in today's workforce with articles like "Don't Let Flextime Get You Laid Off," published in the summer of 2010.

When you work in a company that perpetuates a culture of overwork as the norm, and when you fear losing your job if you don't work more than your designated hours, you may feel pressured to invest all your energy into your company. When you were single, you could put everything into your job because you were responsible only for your own well-being. Now you have a husband, and possibly children, to think about. Taking time away from them to give more to your job, or sharing dinners with your colleagues at the office instead of with your family, will affect all of you. Your relationship will seem like just another job.

If you are spending considerably more time with your colleagues than with your spouse, confiding in them more than in your partner, working on weekends, or traveling frequently on business, it's essential to also set aside time to maintain your marriage.

When it comes to who is most likely to cheat, studies reveal that after seniors, who now have access to sexual enhancement drugs (like Viagra) and who are one of the fastest-growing groups using social media sites, newlyweds are the second-largest demographic that commits adultery. *Women's Health* magazine covered the rise of newlywed infidelity in 2007 after data released by the University of Washington Center for the Study of Health and Risk Behaviors showed that roughly 20 percent of men and 15 percent of women under age 35 admitted to cheating on their spouses (up from 15 and 12 percent, respectively, 15 years earlier).

According to a 2009 study conducted by marriage counselor M. Gary Neuman, an estimated one in 2.7 married men will cheat at some point—and most of their wives will never know about it. But while it is true that more men than women cheat, the gap between the sexes is not as large as you might imagine. Research suggests that approximately 60 percent of cheating is committed by men; 40 percent is committed by women. And research indicates that female infidelity is on the rise.

Women are generally less likely to boast about their sexual partners and are better at deception than men, so many are able to more effectively conceal their affairs. (Attribute it to women's intuition, but women are also more likely to catch a cheating partner than are men.)

Contrary to what many people think, cheating is rarely just about the physical gratification of sex with a new partner. The desire to act out sexually is often a manifestation of more significant problems in a marriage. There are plenty of reasons—many of which can be avoided—that men and women stray.

WHY WE CHEAT

Have you ever thought about cheating on your husband? If so, what drove you to consider it?

People cheat on their spouses for a multitude of reasons—excitement, sex, attention, connection, anger, access, confusion, escape—and often a combination of these factors.

Men and women whose spouses have strayed are sometimes surprised to learn that the person their spouses slept with isn't as physically attractive as they'd imagined. These people wonder why their spouses would have sex with someone who isn't better looking than they are, mistakenly assuming that the act of cheating is purely about attraction and sexual fulfillment.

Of course, in some cases, men and women cheat due to boredom in the bedroom and because they crave the look and feel of a new sexual partner. These people would cite sexual variety as their main motivation for cheating. A former colleague who was cheating on his wife once told me that the thought of being with one woman for the rest of his life made him feel "itchy." I asked him why he got married in the first place, knowing that he would break out in a commitment rash, and he said it was because he was a "family man" and wanted to be married. He loved his wife.

People have different definitions of what constitutes cheating, and when they are covertly having sex with someone outside their marriage, they may make bargains with themselves to justify betraying their spouses. "I'll never sleep overnight with another woman," my ex-colleague told me when we talked about his extramarital relations. He added, "Sleeping is a very intimate act," to explain his rationale.

More often than not, however, cheaters don't cite sex as their primary motivation for straying. There are usually deeper, emotional reasons why people look for sex outside their marriages. According to M. Gary Neuman's research, 92 percent of male cheaters said that their affairs were *not* about sex.

A 40-year-old woman I once interviewed told me that she was so frustrated with the fact that her husband prioritized his work over his family that she wanted to catch his attention by cheating on him with her male friend who was more emotionally available. The end of this story isn't pretty (the male friend actually stopped the affair, and the woman found herself even more devastated and desperate for attention), but in the process she realized that there had been significant problems in her marriage that had gone unaddressed for too long.

Rarely does cheating happen accidentally or without intention. When people say that it "just happened" or that they were "surprised" to have an affair, they fail to acknowledge to others (and to themselves) that there was a conscious motive behind the betrayal. The slippery slope toward infidelity may look innocuous, as the experience my friend's mother recounted about flirting with the cute doctor at work, or it may be well-planned, intentional deceit. But no matter what it looks like or how it starts, every person who cheats makes a choice to cross the line with someone else, and there are usually a number of motives behind this behavior.

In my work with couples, I've seen that attention and approval are two prominent reasons why people enter intimate relationships outside their marriages. In most cases, women are seeking attention and men are looking for approval.

Men who cheat on their wives tend to find sexual partners who offer positive reinforcement and make them feel good about themselves. If a man doesn't sense that his wife approves of his actions or notices his accomplishments, he may also believe he's justified in seeking that approval from someone else. Neuman notes that in cases like these, the other woman makes these guys "feel appreciated, admired . . . men look strong, look powerful and capable; but on the inside, they're insecure like everybody else. They're searching and looking for somebody to build them up and make them feel valued."

Neuman's research supports this. He found that the number-one motive men admitted to for cheating on their wives was feeling "underappreciated" in their marriages. These men were criticized for what they didn't do more than they were complimented for what they contributed. One man I spoke with admitted, "It's tiring to always be told that what you're doing isn't good enough. The woman I had the affair with made me feel good." Without healthy doses of attention, approval, and appreciation at home, many people are likely to seek it elsewhere.

It seems like we could all use a little bit more appreciation these days. According to a recent Gallup poll, 65 percent of working Americans don't feel appreciated in their jobs. Employee satisfaction and performance are largely related to how appreciated employees feel within their companies. In fact, most people polled claimed that being acknowledged and feeling that they were making a positive difference in their organization were as important to their overall job satisfaction as their income and commute. Acknowledgment is one of the cheapest strategies a company can implement, and yet too few managers practice the art of appreciation.

I'll never forget my last day at a job many years ago, when my boss told me that I was one of the best workers she had ever hired. After working at the company for 3 years, I had no idea that I was doing anything more than a satisfactory job (I figured my work was at least okay, as she had a tendency to fire underperforming employees), so I was somewhat surprised. My boss told the person taking over my position, "I couldn't tell Andrea how great she was when she worked with me because then she would have relaxed. I needed to light a fire under her so she'd work hard."

What my boss never realized is that if I had been given positive feedback about my work, I would have worked even harder. I strive to maintain a high standard in my job and, like the employees polled by Gallup, I value and notice words of acknowledgment. That's the beauty of appreciation—it makes most people want to keep up their extraordinary level of performance.

The same principle is true in any relationship, including our marriages. We tend to value positive feedback and perform better when we feel appreciated. Conversely, if we hear only about what we're doing wrong, we are less likely to enjoy our roles as husbands or wives and more inclined to lose interest in pleasing the person offering the constant criticism.

ATTENTION, APPROVAL, AND ADULTERY

As mentioned earlier, women who seek romantic relationships outside their marriages often cite a lack of attention from their husbands as the motive for straying. Many of them believe their husbands no longer listen to them, pay attention to them, or make them feel sexy. I can argue that we, as women, don't need a man to give us any of those things, but we also want our romantic partners to be attracted to us and to enjoy spending time with us. These are perfectly reasonable expectations.

One woman who answered my infidelity questionnaire online and admitted to finding a lover outside her marriage said, "My husband never gives me the 'I want you' eyes that my office mate does. I was hungry for it."

It's clear that women need to feel that they are a priority to their husbands. And when women begin to miss the attention that their partners freely gave them back when they were dating, they may not only be motivated to seek it elsewhere but also believe they're justified in doing so.

EMOTIONAL AFFAIRS

Of course, cheating isn't always physical. By now, you've probably heard the term "emotional affair," which refers to a covert relationship between two people that exhibits a high level of closeness and intimacy but that isn't consummated physically.

Both women and men cheat primarily with people they already know and with whom they have some kind of emotional foundation; however, men are more likely than women to have a sexual affair with a stranger. Men seem better able to compartmentalize their sexual conquests and are therefore more likely than women to cite opportunity or variety as the reason they cheated on their spouses. Women, on the other hand, often create an emotional network when they feel their marriage is threatened and do not cross a physical line with another man until a connection and trust are built.

According to evolutionary psychologist Dr. David M. Buss, "Women have affairs when they're looking to see if there's a better partner out there, with whom they can create a closer love bond." These women may engage in an emotional affair with a male friend who provides support, attention, and understanding.

When we engage in an emotional affair, we're not only craving emotional support from and connection to another man, we're also testing out the waters with him and assessing—from a physical distance—what he might be like as a partner and a provider.

To determine whether or not they are having an emotional affair, married men and women must ask themselves: Am I communicating discreetly with someone outside my marriage? Am I confiding in my crush, more than in my spouse, about personal issues? Would I be comfortable if my spouse overheard my conversations or read the e-mails and texts that I share with the other person?

Even if your relationship with another person is not physical, you may realize you are crossing a loyalty line—especially if you find that you are concealing a relationship with your crush.

CRUSHED

I don't expect that over the span of our marriage, my husband won't look at or fantasize about another woman, but I do expect that he won't act on the desire (unless we have negotiated an open relationship, which is the subject of a different book!). I don't expect that I won't develop crushes on other men, either. When I don't have money to spend, I still like to window-shop. Unless we cut ourselves off from all social interaction, it's unrealistic to believe that any of us will only have eyes for our spouses throughout time.

In many ways, daydreaming and fantasizing about other men are healthy expressions of our sensuality and imagination.

I spoke with my friend Vanessa, who recently became friendly with a man she met at her business school reunion. He asked her, "Why didn't we hang out back in school?" and then flirtatiously mentioned that he regretted not knowing her before she got married.

Vanessa and her former classmate talked about everything from great business ideas they should launch together to personal matters. She said, "There was this connection and electricity between us that I couldn't deny. I was stuck in my head for a few days after that. I had fantasies about him . . . but I feel like I won't go there. I feel very loyal to my husband, and it goes both ways."

I asked her where she gets her strength in those moments when it's tempting to stray. Vanessa responded simply, "I really think it has to do with the respect I have for my husband and for myself. It feels okay to daydream about it, but I don't think I'd actually cross that line, and that's comforting. I trust myself. I can keep it as a fun fantasy."

Every day in our marriages, we make decisions about how we will show up as a partner to our spouses and how we honor the sanctity of our union. Therefore, the question is not "How can I avoid developing a crush on someone else while I'm married?" Rather, it is "What choices will I make, when I have a crush on someone else, to respect my union with my spouse?"

Part of becoming an adult is gaining the ability to practice impulse control. We can foresee the results of our actions, unlike children who do not have the experience or ability to project outcomes. A child may hover around a hot stove until he gets burned and learns that it is dangerous, or she may refuse to go to bed and not realize the next day that's why she's cranky. Children think in terms of immediate wants and don't have the ability to see how their actions affect themselves or others. As adults, we know that our behavior has consequences, and we use this knowledge when we make decisions. We weigh the possible results of our judgment and our actions every day, whether we realize it or not. I don't order the five desserts that sing my name on the menu because I'd like my pants to fit. There are many things I want, but I try to have a degree of impulse control (most of the time, anyway).

The reality is that most married people *will* develop feelings, curiosity, and excitement about other people over the course of their marriages. So how can we make sure that these momentary distractions don't become more than a fleeting crush?

When have you recently practiced impulse control? What did you want to do and what prevented you from doing it?

How to Manage Your Crush

Strategy: Introduce Your Crush to Your Husband

If they don't already know one another, I recommend introducing your husband to your crush. And if they're already acquainted, encourage them to get to know one another better. It may seem counterintuitive to suggest that your husband and your crush become friendly, but the more you see your husband buddy up with a man you've developed an attraction to, and the more your crush sees you interact with your spouse, the less appealing a covert hookup will likely feel to you both. Spending time with your crush and your husband together will help to alleviate the sexual tension between you and the other man, which is a step in the right direction.

Strategy: Remove Yourself from the Situation

What if your crush is a colleague you see every day at work? Asking to be moved to another department, like my friend's mother did, isn't always realistic or the best career strategy. But if removing yourself from the situation is a possibility, consider the cost-benefit analysis. What could it cost you to stay in the situation, and what will it cost you to leave? If the costs of leaving outweigh the costs of staying, make sure to limit your personal exchanges with the object of your affection—that means no fun or flirty e-mails, no texts unrelated to work. Talk to him about great plans with your husband and children, so he knows that you are committed to your family. Avoid private catch-up sessions.

Strategy: Give Your Marriage the Dopamine Boost You Are Craving from Your Crush

Part of what draws you to your crush is the excitement of something new—your interaction with him isn't weighed down by past baggage or influenced by responsibilities at home. In a way, you can be the woman you want to be with your crush—and that can be tempting when you've hit a stale point in life.

Your crush may help you realize that you miss feeling sexy and connecting with your husband the way you used to. We know now that doing novel activities with your husband will give your brain the dopamine high you're craving. We also know that committing to your own creative outlets gives you a boost of passion (and focuses your attention elsewhere).

Reconnect with your sexy self by indulging in your own play—not in play with a crush.

Developing a crush on another man does not necessarily mean you should stray from your marriage; rather, it is likely a sign that you need to break out of your routine. It's time to channel the energy of your passion back into your own life and marriage. If you've experienced a crush on another man, what did you learn about yourself or your husband in the process? What lessons can benefit your marriage?

THE BIG PICTURE

A man who cheated on his wife once told me, "For something that brought me so much pleasure, it was one of the most painful experiences of my life."

When you find yourself flirting with an affair, consider the big picture. When I was in a past relationship and thought about crossing the line with a crush, a girlfriend told me simply, "There are no winners in an affair—everyone gets hurt." So often when people cheat, they think of the immediate gratification and get caught up in the fantasy of the experience. Rarely do we stop to consider how an affair can play out over time. I thought about how pursuing a sexual relationship with another man would eventually add to the confusion of my relationship and ultimately hurt my boyfriend, the other man, and me.

One woman I interviewed offered these reflections on her infidelity: "It's so stupid that I ruined the amazing thing I had for a man who was way less amazing. I wasn't weighing that or considering the consequences of my actions. My relationship with my partner will never be the same."

When I spoke to my friend's mother about the turning point in her 30-year marriage, I asked her how her decision affected her relationship with her husband. Did she ever yearn to be with the other man? She told me that removing herself from the situation was like quitting a bad habit. At first, she craved the high of the crush and the fun of flirting with him. Over time, though, she felt more confident in her relationship with her spouse. She learned about herself and grew as a person. And like anyone who quits an unhealthy habit, she became stronger and in better shape over the years of her marriage as a result. She had chosen her happy ending.

CHAPTER SEVEN

Cheat On Your Husband

(with Your Husband)

Harold Pinter's play *The Lover* opens with a suburban middle-aged husband and wife, Richard and Sarah, getting ready for the day. The mood is flat, and not much is said between them. Moments later, Richard asks his wife if her lover is coming over that afternoon, and she confirms that yes, he is. Richard intimates that he will be seeing his mistress, too, and the two carry on as normal.

When Sarah's husband returns home from work that evening, she is wearing a pretty dress with very high heels and cleaning up the living room. It is clear to the audience and to her husband that her lover spent time with her that afternoon, though she carries on with Richard as if nothing much transpired during the day.

In the following scene, the next day, Sarah transforms into a much sexier version of herself. She moves around her home with a sultry confidence and wears a tight black dress with her high heels. The doorbells rings, and her passionate and artistic lover, Max, enters the scene. Before long, things heat up. They seduce each other, all the while talking about their charged feelings over the elicit affair.

The hook and the intrigue of the play occur when the audience realizes that Max, Sarah's lover, is actually her husband transformed in persona and costume. Sarah, too, looks and moves differently when she's with this version of her spouse. Max and Sarah flirt, argue, tempt, and tease each other.

That evening, Sarah returns to her role as a simple house-wife. She wears a demure dress with flat shoes and prepares Richard a drink while she inquires about his day. Richard, who is back in a basic suit, talks about his tough day at work, and the two carry on as usual.

COURTSHIP ISN'T ONLY FOR DATING

There are days during which I, too, want to have another lover in my home—someone who looks different, touches me differently, and with whom I act like a sexy and spontaneous vixen, totally oblivious to the mountain of dishes in my sink. It's challenging to stay intrigued and seduced in marriage after the dopamine highs have subsided. My husband is a handsome and passionate man, but I know every inch of his body, and he's seen all my angles (including the unflattering ones).

As a dating advice columnist, I witness all of the effort that singles go through to ensure that they will land another date with someone they like. Some of it is uncomfortable to hear (especially when women ask me how to completely change themselves so that the men they are interested in will be inter-ested in them), but sometimes it is . . . dare I say . . . inspiring? Men and women write to ask me how to plan great dates and the best ways to flirt. They are eager to put in effort to capture their dates' interest.

We rarely talk about courting our spouses, but courtship shouldn't be reserved only for the realm of dating. Of course, when we like someone, we try to capture that person's affec-tion and sustain his interest. Shouldn't we try just as hard, or perhaps even harder, to achieve this result in marriage? In some ways, it makes less sense to put forth so much effort to win the affection of virtual strangers, especially since most dates are destined to fail (that's the nature of dating!). Most of the people we try hard to impress and please won't be in our lives for long.

Many women complain that their husbands are no longer romantic, which usually translates to the fact that their husbands are no longer courting them. We have become lazy in this department as well. When was the last time you pursued your husband or he pursued you? How often do you (intentionally) break out of your marriage routine? Do you communicate your needs and desires on a regular basis? Do you put forth a conscious effort to keep one another intrigued?

If you can't answer yes to these questions but admit that you've been tempted to cross the line with other men, you may want to think again and consider cheating on your husband—*with* your husband. Feeling bored and uninspired in your marriage may motivate you to seek excitement with someone else, but that's not going to solve your problem. If you're experiencing the blahs in your marriage, take it as a cue that it's time to shake up your routine.

Chances are you're not regularly experiencing the fun and excitement that was part of your everyday life with your husband when he was your boyfriend. You may miss feeling like a seductress, you may yearn for the ways you and he used to taunt and tease each other, or you may reminisce about how silly and fun you both were when you hung out.

When we started dating, Michael and I would plan adventures like searching for the best pizza slice in the city, and we'd log our results in a spreadsheet with appropriate categories for sauce, cheese, and quality of crust. We'd spend weekends exploring new areas of town and random hole-in-the-wall restaurants. We'd kiss each other on park benches and dare each other to do silly things in public. I think back to those moments with nostalgia and some surprise (how did we have energy for all of that?), but I also know that being adventurous is still in us.

Recently, Michael and I went to Santa Monica and paid homage to one of our favorite guilty pleasures, the TV show *Three's Company*. Michael turned on his phone's video feature and we shot our own version of the opening credits on the beach boardwalk. That night, we stayed up editing the piece and cutting it to the show's theme song. We could barely wait to share it on YouTube. We woke up snuggling and laughing about the project. During this goofy experience, I was brought back in time—not to the early '80s, when I first watched *Three's Company*, but to 2005, when Michael and I decided to turn our friendship into a romantic relationship and spent time making each other smile.

Dating your husband is essential to a healthy marriage. And one of the most exciting parts of dating is the sexual intrigue and attraction that keep you coming back for more. If you haven't expressed your sensuality since you were dating, you may also miss this part of yourself. After all, you're not just a wife, a worker, or a mother—you are a woman.

My friend Jen, who has been married to her husband, Jim, for 7 years, admits that while she loves her current life as a wife and mother, she misses seeing herself as a sexy, "womanly" woman. It's not only Jim who fell in love with that girl—in many ways, Jen was in love with her, too. She felt confident and happy when she was connected to her sensual self. She loved feeling sexy and knowing that men were attracted to her. While she doesn't want to emulate her single days, she does wonder how she can reclaim that missing piece of herself in a way that is practical, accessible, and appealing.

WHAT I LEARNED FROM A CALL GIRL

As the author of *Diary of a Manhattan Call Girl,* Tracy Quan is one of Manhattan's most famous (or infamous) former call girls. Today, she advocates on behalf of women who make their living in the sex industry.* I called her recently to ask her opinion on why married men have sex with escorts and what prompts these men to become repeat clients.

Tracy said that a common request by men visiting sex workers is something called the "GFE." I had to stop her and ask for translation (it sounded like a standardized test).

Tracy explained that the GFE stood for the Girlfriend Experience. "We've done this for years, but now some people in the sex industry are trying to make it more commercial, so they put a name on it," she remarked.

When a man requests a GFE, he wants to experience a more well-rounded exchange than strictly sex. For some customers, this means holding hands and kissing the women they have hired, or booking women who will talk to them, touch them, and make them feel young again. Sex is usually involved (and oral sex is a common component of the GFE), but it is not calculated on the clock. In fact, this service isn't bound by time requirements, so the customer can feel relaxed and as if he is in a relationship. Many men who order a GFE are interested in exploration without judgment or discussing their lives in a relaxed environment. The exchange between the man and the woman participating in the GFE is generally sweet and kind, as it would be if they were dating, and cuddling is common.

I was intrigued. Fascinated. I wanted to order a GFE (or offer a GFE, I wasn't sure). I also wondered why we married women

---

*There are a number of female sex workers who have entered the trade and have been driven to work in the industry for reasons that are anything but empowered, but Tracy and her friends— who advocate on behalf of sex workers' rights—strongly defend their choice and right to work in one of the world's oldest professions.

rarely offer our husbands one of the most popular call girl services and why we can't ask our husbands to give us the BFE.

KISS AND TELL

Kissing is a part of the GFE, for good reason. When we are dating, we often spend hours with locked lips; when we are married, we usually spend mere minutes (or, perhaps more accurately, seconds) kissing.

Most of us remember our first kiss. Mine was at 14 years old in the front seat of my 16-year-old boyfriend's car. He leaned in and put his hand on my knee, and we both started to tremble. I had practiced for years on my pillow, but this was different. His kiss literally took my breath away (I started to cough at the start); before we knew it, we had been in that front seat for over an hour and it was past my curfew. In those days, all I did with boyfriends was kiss, but I never tired of it. I looked forward to the good-night smooch at the end of each date (or in the back of the movie theater, in some cases). It was intoxicating.

Anthropologists have found that 90 percent of the world shows affection, friendship, love, and lust through kissing. In 10 percent of the world's cultures (among many African tribes, for example), kissing is uncommon. For Westerners, romantic kissing is often the first expression of sexual and/or loving feelings for someone and is one of the easiest ways to trigger the pleasure centers of our brains. A 2008 article in the magazine *Scientific American* notes: "A kiss triggers a cascade of neural messages and chemicals that transmit tactile sensations, sexual excitement, feelings of closeness, motivation, and even euphoria."

When we think back to dating our husbands, we often remember the first kiss we shared (and how amazing and seductive it was!) but can't recall the last time we had a passionate kiss with our husbands for fun. Few married couples kiss for longer than seconds during the day, and a number of women I have interviewed admit that they don't even kiss during sex.

My friend Sarah says that she kisses her husband daily, but kissing her spouse the same way she kisses her kids on their way out of the house for school wasn't the kind of smooch I was inquiring about.

Before you and your husband were married, you used kissing to connect, express your feelings for one another, and heighten the sexual mood. Kissing in those days was one of the first and most powerful ways you shared emotional and physical intimacy. Granted, everything was new and exciting about your exchanges with your partner then. You weren't used to the way he touched you, tasted, and smelled.

Geraldine, the mother of two boys under age 6, says she regrets that she and her husband have stopped kissing. She recently felt inspired to make out with him after watching a kissing contest on a reality television show. Following the rules of the TV contest, she blindfolded her husband and set a timer so that they could have a full 2 minutes of kissing—"with tongue!" she added. "It was so fun and sexy," she said. "He and I forget how much we love kissing. Our make-out session kind of started as a joke but quickly reignited feelings. I felt weak in the knees."

Kissing is one of the easiest ways for you and your husband to give each other the GFE and the BFE without putting in too much time or work. See if you can kiss your husband for at least 30 uninterrupted seconds and notice how much of a spark you can create—in less than a minute.

TALK TECHY TO ME

A pet peeve for many daters is that the men they are seeing refuse to pick up the phone to chat or to ask them out. One client wrote me with this recommendation: "TELL MEN NOT TO TEXT IF THEY WANT TO SEE ME AGAIN." (I assume she was screaming her request.)

Modern dating is full of e-courtship—text messages, Facebook pokes, and e-mail flirtations. In Chapter 6, we explored the significant role that technology plays in aiding cheaters to connect discreetly with their lovers. Sexy texts (which you probably know by now are referred to as "sexts") and flirty e-mail exchanges are often the way temptation is initially sparked and communication is concealed.

Married couples tend to use technology for far more practical purposes, like coordinating plans and figuring out family logistics. There's nothing sexy about planning schedules and sending grocery lists via SMS. Few of us have leveraged technology in our marriages to heighten anticipation and excitement the way daters (and cheaters) often do, even though these networks are readily available and require little effort.

Sending a flirty e-mail or a text message is a great way to communicate your feelings of desire without the pressure or embarrassment you may feel about saying them out loud. It might feel silly at first, but when your husband sees your suggestive note or sexy photo on his cell phone in the middle of a slow day at work, the results are usually well worth the few seconds it took you to compose and send. This simple act will get both of your minds racing and inject a little fun into what may otherwise be a boring or stressful afternoon. I'm a big fan of tech talk as a means to whet the sexual appetite and build a little intrigue in marriage.

For those of you who are new to sexting, here's a few basics to consider:

○ Sext in the affirmative.

Consider starting your sext with "I want . . ." or "I love when you . . ." There's nothing sexy about a wishy-washy text or one that uses negativity. (Therefore, stay away from phrases like: "We haven't hooked up in a while. Let's try to later.")

○ Consider your approach.

Do you want to be playful or provocative? An overt text may read: "I want you to make love to me tonight as soon as the kids go to sleep. I'll be naked and waiting for you in our room . . . ." A more subtle text would hint at the action without going into details, "I hope you have energy tonight. I'm planning on offering you a fantastic dessert post-dinner . . ."

○ Be discreet.

If your kids or others have access to your phone, delete messages or store them elsewhere once received. This is especially true if you are sharing provocative photos!

And a note about e-flirting—it doesn't always have to be sexual. When Michael and I e-flirt, we often send funny or sweet photos via e-mail or text to show what we're seeing that day or what's on our minds. I'll e-mail him a photo of something that reminds me of an inside joke we share or a shot of the restaurant I want us to try. Sending these messages is a way to demonstrate that we are thinking about each other. These texts are usually frivolous—and that's why they're fun.

KEEP DOORS CLOSED IN YOUR MARRIAGE

Bet you don't hear that marriage advice often, do you? When I refer to "keeping doors closed in marriage," I mean literally—and figuratively.

A number of women are so comfortable with their husbands that they share bathroom space in every conceivable way. Of course, sometimes it's necessary to hop in the shower while your husband is shaving at the sink, or brush your teeth while he's in the shower, but there are many bathroom habits your husband does not need to see (and vice versa). One woman I know analyzes her unwanted body fat in front of her husband, pointing out how her arms jiggle every chance she gets. None of us would dare do these things if we were still dating our husbands (at least, I hope not).

Geraldine and her husband have two young kids and very busy careers. They find that keeping all doors open (even when using the toilet) is more efficient, since they need to save time in the morning and every minute counts. Geraldine admitted, "It's common for one of us to be taking a shower while the other is going number two." When I looked horrified, she said in defense of her open-door toilet policy, "I don't need to hide anything from my husband. We're really close. I don't need to pretend I don't have bowel movements!"

I understand where she's coming from. Your husband has seen everything, so hiding something from him or acting modest in front of him may seem pointless. If you've given birth and he was beside you, he's probably seen more of you than you've seen yourself!

It's great to be comfortable around your husband, and it may seem strange to create physical barriers when you know one another's bodies so well. But think of it this way: How do you feel when you witness him doing things that are kind of gross? When you see him clipping his toenails or trimming his nose hairs, do you feel attracted to him? If you find that you're not feeling as sexy as you were when you were dating, a good first step for both of you may be to close the bathroom door and reserve viewings of your naked bodies for the bedroom.

In one of my favorite *Seinfeld* episodes, Jerry dates a woman who does mundane tasks while naked—like eating waffles and playing board games and opening jars. Jerry was attracted to her but realizes that there's "good naked" and "bad naked."

It may sound extreme, but I don't get dressed or undressed in front of my husband. I'm not prudish about nudity—I have no problem blow-drying my hair at the gym with a towel around my waist or taking my clothes off in a dressing room with a friend while shopping, but nudity in that context is different than being naked around the man I am intimate with.

Since it is difficult to sustain intrigue and an element of mystery in marriage, I made a conscious decision when Michael and I moved in together not to walk around our home uncovered. When my husband sees my body, it is something he hasn't seen in a while (hopefully not too long a while!). Like Seinfeld, I believe in sharing the "good naked."

Tracy Quan agreed with my "no naked unless we're getting down" approach and added another piece of advice that she borrows from the trade. She once heard another well-known sex worker, Xaviera Hollander (author of *The Happy Hooker*), instruct women not to leave underwear lying around in the presence of their clients. The point of concealing underclothes is to make the whole sexual experience about fantasy and novelty. Hollander's perspective, a lesson she says she got from her mother, is that even underwear should be reserved for special occasions. So, when your man takes off your bra, it's not one he has seen hanging to dry in the shower. That way, the whole experience, from the first moment he touches you, will feel fresh.

Keep Some Doors Closed (Figuratively)

Keeping communication open, so that you and your husband feel comfortable confiding in each other without judgment, is an essential piece of a healthy relationship, but neither of you needs to know about the minutiae of each other's day. You don't need to hear about whether or not his hair seems thinner this week, and he certainly doesn't want to hear you complain about your body every time you feel fat. (If you keep pointing it out, in fact, he will start to notice it. Don't you love that? People tend to notice what we tell them about ourselves!)

Not everything you or your husband feels like venting or gossiping about has to be shared with each other (that's what friends are for!). Just as you don't want to hear every detail of the rules of his fantasy football league, he probably doesn't care to know the details of your friend's most recent drama. If you both recycle your insights about these topics regularly, you're prone to start tuning one another out, which is not a good habit to fall into.

EXPRESS YOUR SENSUAL SIDE

Pleasure is the object, duty, and the goal of all rational creatures.
—Voltaire

What does it mean to be your *sensual self?*

Sensuality involves connecting with your senses so that you are fully aware of smells, textures, tastes, and sounds. Living sensually is about expressing your passions and participating in activities that bring you pleasure. Your definition of what sensuality looks like may be different from mine.

If I am indulging in a few bites of a warm molten chocolate cake, or immersed in good music, I feel sensual. (Not surprisingly, these experiences tap the pleasure centers of the brain, just as sex does.) I also express sensuality through my body. Feeling delicate fabrics on my skin or getting a massage sparks my sensual self.

One aspect of sensuality is embracing a feeling of guilt-free indulgence—letting go of what you *should* do (and keeping the experience in your head) in favor of what you *want* to do (and letting the experience permeate your body and soul).

It's not easy to connect with your sensual self when you have family and work obligations that demand your attention in very practical ways. There's nothing sexy about doing housework (though one of my friends swears that she gets in a sensual zone while doing dishes), feeding your kids, or sitting through a 2-hour meeting.

People who are committed to a sensual life find moments to indulge their senses and are generally happier as a result. Even though it's unrealistic to be sensual every moment of every day, connecting with this part of yourself on a regular basis should be a priority in your life and in your marriage.

For you, living sensually may consist of paying $10 for a 10-minute massage when you don't have time or money for more, or having a glass of crisp Chardonnay with dinner, or drawing yourself a warm bath before bedtime. Any activity that helps you snap out of the "to-do" mode in favor of "to be" is a good start.

PLAN TO BE SPONTANEOUS

When you were dating your spouse, you probably had little regard for time (when you are falling in love, time feels suspended, in fact). You could come and go as you pleased, and you were not accountable to anybody.

I often instruct singles to approach dating as they approach a vacation. On vacation, we're generally open to stepping outside our comfort zones, we are present in the moment, and we let ourselves relax and have fun. Even though taking a trip requires planning, once you are away from home, you allow for some spontaneity (or at least I hope so).

In your day-to-day life, it may seem impossible to capture the easygoing spirit of a vacation. When you are on deadline for work, or if you have young children who are restless, or if you face a stack of bills and paperwork when you get home, it's more difficult to put on your vacation hat. On date night, though, you can.

Whether it's your first date or your hundredth with the same person, being your "vacation self" on a date still works. There's little room for pure spontaneity in marriage, but that doesn't mean you can't plan moments of it (I realize that sounds like a contradiction). If you have a 3-hour date blocked off, you may have a dinner reservation at 8:00, but why not see where the night takes you after that? Choose an area of town you are less familiar with so you can explore something new together. You can be present in the experience on your night together and channel your inner vacation alter egos.

I met Sonali at a Halloween party. She and her husband were dressed in costume and acting like giddy teenagers on a date. She has two kids, including one with special needs, but the night I met her she told me they took advantage of her mom's visit from out of town and decided to have fun and hit the town together. She said, "On a regular basis, my husband and I hire help so that we can keep up the spontaneity that has always made our relationship fun. Sometimes I'll buy last-minute tickets to a show or exhibit, and we'll just go for it. These things don't require as much organization as people think."

Eighty-year-old Carol told me that she and her husband used to check into a hotel or a motel at least once a month and pretend they were having an affair. They stayed in bed for hours cuddling, reading the paper together, and smooching like they did when they first met.

"All excuses are nonsense," she said. "There's no time? No kidding—so make time!" Even when money was tight, Carol found a way to hire a sitter to watch her kids so she could go for lunch with friends and on dates with her husband. She created a structure for her vacation self, and her sensual self, to be expressed.

PURSUE, PURSUE, PURSUE!

The elements of sensuality, spontaneity, and the GFE would be present in a relationship if you were having a seductive affair or had just started dating someone new. Now that you've been in a relationship for years with one person, you may miss the mystery, intrigue, and courtship that you used to have with your partner. Earlier I wrote about the Ps of dating and marriage; now I want to introduce another important P: Pursue!

If you miss feeling excited about your husband the way you used to, pursuing him by incorporating small gestures, like sexting and kissing, can reignite the connection. And if you want *him* to pursue *you* more actively, encourage him with your response. Show him how happy you are when he offers you the BFE and plans interesting dates; talk to him about how much you love it when he notices the effort you put in to look good. Even if it's as simple as saying, "I love it when you tell me I look hot in my red dress"—let him know that his pursuit keeps your spark alive.

Being aware of your senses and indulging in activities that bring you pleasure are two of the easiest, and sexiest, ways to express yourself in your otherwise overbooked schedule. Keep in mind that indulgences are measured by quality—not quantity. A quick massage—or a quickie—may inspire you to try more.

What parts of your sexy and sensual self have you not shared lately? If you crave hanging out with the woman your husband fell in love with—it's time to find her again.

CHAPTER EIGHT

Let's Talk about Sex

At a bachelorette brunch I attended recently with mostly married girlfriends, one woman burst out and asked the group, "How often do you have sex with your husbands?" She mentioned it as casually as she might have interrupted to ask, "Can you please pass the sugar?"

Everyone at the table laughed, but it soon became clear that all of the women were listening. Most admitted that they wanted to know if their monthly average was normal or if they should be concerned (or pleased).

How often do you think the average American married couple has sex each month? If you took into account the number of jokes about the role of sex in marriage, you might assume that the answer would be "none." If you asked your married girlfriends about their sex lives, you might begin to worry that your monthly average is way below normal.

In social conversations, people often share different numbers about their intimate lives than they do in more intimate conversations.

According to a recent survey conducted by the National Opinion Research Center at the University of Chicago, American married couples report to having sex 68.5 times a year, or slightly more than once a week. Our lives may be busier than ever, but according to the center's data, the statistics haven't changed much over the past decade. Studies also note that married people have more sex than singles, on average, although recent estimates point to the fact that 41 percent of Americans report to be in sexless marriages.

At the brunch table, I heard numbers ranging from "almost every day" to "I can hardly remember." One or two times a week was common; but there was no *normal*, even in this small sample of 11 women.

In reality, "normal" is the frequency dictated only by you and your spouse. Have you ever asked your husband how often he would like to be intimate, what time of day he prefers for a make-out session (including whether or not there's a time after which he won't be receptive), or where he enjoys having sex? Have you ever scheduled a romp? Perhaps it seems counterintuitive to craft a sex schedule the way you would decide who should pick up the dry cleaning or get the kids from practice, but like everything else in your partnership, sex has to be discussed and negotiated. Without open and honest communication about your sex life, resentments can build up.

According to a recent *Women's Health* article, "A man would rather have basic sex a few times a week than swinging-from-the-chandeliers sex every once in a while." Of course, there are always exceptions. Not all men want to have sex frequently, just as not all women are always in the mood.

If you and your spouse have the exact same sexual appetite and enjoy all of the same things in the bedroom, consider yourself among the lucky few. If not, it's important to have a conversation about what you want your sex life to look like—and take action—so that you both feel sexually fulfilled and expressed.

Even though you share most things with your husband, talking about sex with him may feel awkward and unnatural, but it's essential to be proactive with this aspect of your relationship together so that hurt feelings or resentments don't manifest. When you and your partner are not on the same page sexually, insecurities or anxieties are bound to come up for both of you.

If you feel too uncomfortable to discuss your sex life face-to-face, you may want to ask your husband questions about his needs and desires one night in bed when the lights are out.

One woman in attendance at the bachelorette brunch offered her very practical approach to sex with her husband. She said, "You know how parking meter officers have to fill a monthly ticket quota in order to keep their jobs? I have a quota each month that I try to fill, too. I get nervous if I don't make my numbers."

Many of the women at the table agreed and talked about their own scoring system. I couldn't believe it. Sex is calculated and measured? It seems as if many women can go without sex and not miss it, which begs the question: Why don't they have the desire? I've known women who desperately crave pizza when they cut back on carbs . . . . Shouldn't they miss sex when they go without? Geraldine, another woman at the brunch table, said she was inspired by an article she read that likened sex to exercise. She remarked, "I don't ever feel like going to the gym, but after I go, I'm always glad I did. I feel the same way about sex."

Of course, some women love and crave sex with their spouses and have sex with them often. But for women who are not sexually interested, reasons for not having sex include lack of time (as noted in Chapter 5, most mothers I interviewed admitted that they would rather take a nap than have a sexy rendezvous), not feeling "in the mood" after spending a long day at work or a day with the kids, and not enjoying sex. One woman at the brunch admitted, "Sex does nothing for me—I do it only for my husband." It was a sentiment shared by too many women at the table.

A sex therapist and founder of the online site GoodInBed.com, Dr. Ian Kerner notes that this feeling is common among married women, particularly mothers. He remarked, "Having kids is a tremendous milestone that really takes a lot out of a relationship. One study out of the University of Denver showed that upward of 90 percent of women experience declines in relationship satisfaction once they become parents. It's common for any couple in a long-term relationship, especially women, to want to want sex but not really have the desire."

It seems that if women could get more pleasure and satisfaction from having sex with their husbands, their desire for it would increase. Enjoying sex doesn't necessarily mean experiencing an orgasm (or multiple orgasms) every single time you get between the sheets. What's pleasurable in bed is different for every woman, but each woman needs to know what makes her feel good.

DO YOU LIKE YOUR BODY AS MUCH AS YOUR HUSBAND DOES?

What's the first word that comes to mind when you think of your body? When you look in the mirror, do you like what you see?

The sad reality is that most women have a long list of (perceived) physical faults with their bodies. Very few women look at their reflections and think "hot girl!"

Most of us have body parts that we're not happy with and try to camouflage or hide. In fact, a shocking 97 percent of women polled by *Glamour* magazine in early 2011 said they had "I hate my body" thoughts every single day. (The study found that these women had negative thoughts about their body 13 times daily.) We worry about parts of our bodies that most people probably don't notice (that is, if we don't point out our flaws to them).

I don't need to tell you that the Photoshopped, airbrushed, and digitally retouched images of women in the media are unrealistic. But even though we know those bodies don't reflect reality, many of us aspire to look like the women we see in magazines and on television. I've heard celebrities admit that they wished they looked more like the version they see of themselves in print! It's difficult to walk by another magazine cover highlighting the best and worst bikini bodies and not think about how you compare, but one key aspect of good sex is embracing your sexy hot self. (Don't blush, I know she's in there.) Feeling good in your skin is directly related to being good in bed, since good sex requires getting out of your head, letting go of your inhibitions, and demonstrating confidence. The alternative—feeling insecure or uncomfortable in your own skin—can negatively affect your sex life.

I spoke with Jan, who admitted that she's felt insecure about her body since having her son 2 years ago. She has a long list of physical changes she wishes she could make, and she avoids shopping for clothes because she finds it depressing to try things on. "You have a baby and your body changes," she said. "After my pregnancy, I had hair where I didn't want it and lost hair where I like it. I can't wear my skinny jeans—those are for skinny people. I don't even recognize myself. I'd love to say it doesn't matter because I have a beautiful son, but I want to be beautiful, too. I'm down on myself, and it's not only affecting me. My husband is affected, too."

The messages you tell yourself about your body do affect your sex life and your marriage. Not only do you feel less sexy when you don't feel good about yourself, but there's nothing particularly hot about a woman who can't stop obsessing about every inch of her physique. My friend Trina mentioned that she can't blame motherhood on her lack of sexual desire or energy, since she's been married for only 3 years and has no children.

She admitted, "I'm in a job where I sit all day, so I feel like a blob when I get home from work. The last thing I want to do is take off my clothes and have sex." Trina used to initiate sex, and now she often avoids it since she's tired and feels "gross." She misses the playful and confident woman she was a few years ago and is ready to invite her back into her bedroom. "I want to feel sexy again. I want to enjoy sex but I don't know how," she said. I offered the "fake it until you make it" approach and suggested that she channel the seductive woman she used to be. I asked her to imagine how she would approach sex with her husband, even after a stressful week at the office, during the first year of dating him. She laughed at my suggestion and then said, "Damn, I was sexy."

A male friend once told me that when he gets naked with a woman, he's not thinking, "She really needs to lose 5 pounds!" He's thinking, "Yay! Sex!" If your man's not thinking about your flaws, why should you?

Life coaches and therapists often refer to the source of negative self-talk as "the gremlin," because when your mental chatter is full of self-criticism, it is as if there is a monster stuck in your head. You probably wouldn't tell your good friend (or perhaps even your worst enemy) some of the mean things you tell yourself.

One way to battle the gremlin is to identify what it's telling you (i.e., "your thighs are so gross") and choose to respond to the attack with a sincere compliment.

Or when it starts to criticize a body part you don't like, consciously shift your focus to a part of your body that you love.

One client told me how she hated her "huge hips." I asked her to quickly switch her attention, without thinking about it, to a part of her body that she liked. She said, "I have amazing breasts," and then a moment later (unsolicited) she added, ". . . and anyway, my hips make me a woman!" It's as if the gremlin was kicked out of the picture as soon as she shifted her focus.

Adopt a new mantra about your body. If you've been telling yourself for years that you look bad naked and need to lose weight, replace the message with something empowering like "My curves make me a woman," "I'm going to get in shape because I want to be even stronger," or "I love my toned arms and legs." Find something that resonates with you and your self-image. Try a few new mantras about your body on for size (excuse the pun), and then repeat your positive mantra when you look in the mirror, when you get naked, and (silently) when you get it on with your partner. With time, patience, and practice, the gremlin is less likely to make an appearance in your bedroom.

ANATOMY 101

Liking your body is one thing; knowing it is another. So how well *do* you know your body? Many women who don't enjoy sex admit that they haven't spent much time examining and touching their bodies in recent years. A doctor I interviewed told me that she's surprised by how few of her female patients know about their own anatomy.

Dr. Betty Anne Dodson, author of the best-selling *Sex for One* and the recent *Betty Dodson: My Sexual Revolution,* is widely known as the Grandmother of Masturbation. She's unlike most 82-year-old women you know, I'm guessing. She signs her e-mails "BAD" and has been teaching masturbation workshops for decades. She leads provocative discussions about sex and play on her Web site and has dedicated her career to teaching women and men how to pleasure themselves and each other. I thought she would be the perfect person to call with my queries "Why aren't more married women enjoying sex? And what can they do?"

Dr. Dodson responded to my questions by acknowledging the challenges of being sexy *and* being a mom. "Very few people realize the amount of work that goes into raising children," she remarked. "Most mothers are too exhausted to enjoy sex with their partners when they are supposed to have an orgasm, too. We take much longer to get off, and it can seem like another job." We may also feel pressured to show our husbands that we are still turned on by them and that they are sexually satisfying us.

Dr. Dodson advises women to find time during the day (such as during their children's naptime) to get out their vibrators and "enjoy an orgasm." Or, she added, "After they have sex with their husbands, women can give themselves their own orgasms, providing they know how to pleasure themselves." If you feel uncomfortable with the idea of masturbation, consider this: According to a 2010 report compiled by the Kinsey Institute, more than half of women surveyed between the ages of 18 to 49 said that they had masturbated during the previous 3 months.

Dr. Dodson encourages women to embrace masturbation as something that's not only fun but good for the health of our bodies and the health of our sexual relationships. "Masturbation is our first natural sexual activity," she explained. "It's how we discover and develop our sexual responses in order to enjoy positive, good feelings."

(UH) OHHHH . . .

Most women I've interviewed claim that achieving orgasm with their partners is a priority, but research shows that a number of women do not regularly climax through intercourse. Most women need direct clitoral stimulation (manually or orally) to climax, and even then, some women aren't able to experience an orgasm. According to a 2010 poll conducted by *Cosmopolitan* magazine, 71 percent of women admitted to pretending to have orgasms (though only 30 percent of men believed women faked it!).

I asked psychiatrist and sex therapist Dr. Frank Sommers, of the goodsexnetwork.com, about the fake orgasm phenomenon among women. He remarked, "Nobody readily admits to faking orgasms, so it's difficult to know the 'real' numbers. The only thing we do know is that there is a gap between men and women and what they perceive. For example, in a recent study 85 percent of men reported that their partners had orgasms but only 64 percent of the women (who were their partners) reported [having] orgasms."

There is clearly a discrepancy between what men perceive and what women actually experience between the sheets. We must be great performers! Perhaps, though, we're not fooling anyone but ourselves.

So—what is an orgasm?

According to Dr. Sommers, an orgasm is a feeling, sensation, and overall release that is usually accompanied by intense pleasure. (He notes that there are exceptions to this; for example, there are men who ejaculate but don't experience pleasure.)

While different people experience orgasms differently, the basic response is the same for men and women. When a person becomes sexually aroused, blood flow increases to his or her pelvic region and the muscles in that area contract to release the tension. For women, our state of emotional and mental arousal is also integral to our ability to climax.

Dr. Ian Kerner explained the three steps to the neurophysiological reaction that a woman experiences when she orgasms:

1. Blood flow increases to her genitals.

2. She experiences muscular tension throughout her entire body. A certain element of requisite sexual tension eventually triggers pelvic contractions.

3. She is able to deactivate and relax her mind. Dr. Kerner notes that it is more difficult for women to get into this zone, and if there is a change in the type of stimulation around her, she may lose her state of arousal. In addition, a woman's body image and self-esteem are factors in her ability to achieve an orgasm. In women, there is a strong mind-body connection, whereas men can have a sexual response based on visual cues and other physical stimuli.

Sex educator Amy Levine, of IgniteYourPleasure.com, offers these tips for those who are O-challenged:

○ Make a to-do list of all the stuff that's floating around in your head—anything that can distract you from being in the moment. Relax.

○ Get naked, look at your vulva in a mirror, and explore your body on your own. You have to know what feels good and express it to your partner (either verbally or by showing him or her what you like) in order for him or her to begin to figure out how to get you off.

○ Use water-based lube, as wetter can feel better.

○ Know that most women need clitoral stimulation to climax.

○ Take the focus away from having an orgasm and enjoy the sensations. If not, you'll likely sabotage your satisfaction.

○ During sex, get into positions like doggie-style or you-on-top that easily allow for clitoral touch. (Bonus: It's helpful to use a small bullet-shaped vibrator between the two of you.)

○ Realize that orgasms can be as short and simple as feeling like a sneeze or earth-shattering and moan-worthy. And they can vary from one encounter to the next. It's totally natural not to have an orgasm every time you have sex.

According to former Manhattan call girl Tracy Quan, one of the biggest misconceptions people have about paid sexual transactions is that they always resemble something you'd see in a porn movie. "I'm not an acrobat!" she joked. She said that most clients aren't looking for crazy, fetishy sex (though those clients certainly exist); many just want to experience the fantasy of sex without feeling the pressures of everyday life. They want to enjoy sex in an atmosphere that is fun, seductive, and open.

"Most people need more than one kind of sex to be satisfied. One day, a guy may crave the GFE (Girlfriend Experience) and the next, the PSE (Porn Star Experience)," Quan remarked. It's good to introduce variety, to taunt, and to tease—just as people do when they are dating or cheating. Quan was frank about the fact that most sex workers are playing a role when they have sex, just as some girlfriends and wives are.

You don't always have to be in the mood to get into the mood.

Amy Levine concurs that even though sex was fun and exciting early in your relationship (perhaps you and your partner took pride in your sexy connection), it is completely normal for sex to become monotonous over time. Even if your sexual spark is now dwindling (or barely flickering), "the key is to remember that the spark was once there, and rekindle the fire by making an effort to keep it interesting," said Levine. "Partners need to express how they're feeling, break out of their routine, and be more adventurous (and this doesn't have to include activities that are out of one's comfort zone)."

Dr. Sommers shared another suggestion, one he encourages in his practice. "People have to practice better verbal intercourse—talking and listening—because this builds a bridge to sexual intimacy. Also, variation is important, since people are creatures of habit. Variety in time and place of lovemaking is good—maybe a 'passion weekend' would work. How you dress can also impact desire."

DRESS UP (OR DOWN)

Monica is an Orthodox Jewish woman who answered my anonymous sex survey online. She and her husband believe in taking risks in the bedroom (and outside of it!). She told me that their intimate life gets better every year. She also mentioned how much she enjoys dressing up and using costumes: "If I see my husband get excited by a cheerleader, or if we see a movie about something and he's into it, I go out and I buy that outfit. I have fun with it!"

Of course, not all women feel as comfortable as Monica about dressing up for sex. Monica suggested starting with a simple accessory, like a boa or a pair of sexy heels, and experimenting with how you feel. A few risqué details can introduce a new level of passion to your regular routine. "What I've realized is that it doesn't really matter what you wear," she says. "You can wear a garbage bag in bed, and if you feel good about yourself in that, your husband will probably be into it, too." (Especially since the point is for the attire to come off, anyway!) But keep in mind that costumes are fun only if they work for you. They can be counterproductive if they make you uncomfortable. (I know a couple who said there was nothing that killed mood faster than their awkward attempt at role-playing.)

Another way Monica and her husband keep their sexual routine interesting is by finding a few days each month to refrain from touching each other. During this time, even nonsexual contact like hugs or holding hands is avoided. Monica and her partner practice no touching because of their adherence to a Jewish custom (one in which a husband and wife don't touch each other during a window of time each month), but she believes it creates healthy sexual tension and excitement that she and her husband can leverage. She added, "I think this lack of touch makes sex more beautiful and makes us want each other a little more. A period of abstinence every month makes you build your communication." Being conscious of *not* touching may provoke you to crave it a little more.

Introducing variety may be a simple tweak, like switching up the order of foreplay, initiating the act of sex with your spouse instead of expecting him to do so, or choosing a completely different area of your home for a make-out session. In a sense, you are role-playing when you approach your routine differently.

One of the easiest ways to change things up is to wear something to bed that makes you feel sexy.

I'm embarrassed to admit that I have underwear in my drawer that should have been thrown out years ago. One pair of cotton panties, a sad and faded version of the color purple, has a rip in the back—but because these panties are so comfortable, I haven't been able to part with them since I first started wearing them in the mid-'90s. (This pair, in fact, looks like it belongs to someone in her mid-nineties.) I would be mortified if anyone other than my husband saw these. So why would I keep something that I would be embarrassed for anyone else to see . . . and wear them around my lover?

Many of us have secret underclothes that we know should have gone to lingerie heaven years ago. We may be stubborn enough to keep them, but I hope we're smart enough not to wear them when we want to get intimate with our husbands. If you were dating someone new, or cheating with a lover, you probably wouldn't wear granny panties. You'd wear underwear that made you feel confident and sexy.

Like everything sensual, wearing nice lingerie isn't only for your partner's benefit.

Challenge: Go shopping or excavate the pretty bra and underwear you bought for a trip or a special occasion. Wear it under your clothes for a week and see how you feel. You may be surprised by the power of the panties.

MORE SEX = LESS STRESS

Apart from being fun and pleasurable, studies show that women demonstrate a decrease in stress response when they are sexually active. This finding may seem counterintuitive. I know that when I'm stressed, the thought of taking off my clothes (and exerting any kind of energy) is unappealing. But with physical affection and activity, our bodies demonstrate an increase in the "love" hormone oxytocin and a decrease in the stress hormone cortisol. This response is good for both our physical and emotional state.

Dr. Kerner notes that one of the trouble spots for couples he counsels occurs when they go longer than a week without intercourse. He said, "There's truth to the phrase 'use it or lose it.' When you stop having sex or go a long time without it, both men and women's testosterone levels lower, and we actually get habituated and used to the rut."

He suggests that couples initiate sexual activity even when they don't feel like being sexual together. "Let your body lead and your mind will follow," he advises. "Make time for intimacy. So many people say they don't have time but spend hours checking Facebook or surfing the Internet at night before they head to bed. They don't prioritize intimacy and collapse into bed. If they go too long without sex, before they know it, more time passes and they can't remember the last time they had sex." In other words, if you create a pattern of avoiding sex, it can be hard to break the cycle.

It's probably not surprising that married couples who report being happy with their sex lives report more satisfaction in their relationships overall. As television talk show host Dr. Phil says, when sex is good between partners, it accounts for about 10 percent of a relationship—but when it's not, it counts for about 90 percent of a relationship. If you have more serious sexual incompatibility issues, or if you or your husband has a medical condition that affects intimacy, consider seeking professional guidance. It is truly an investment in your future.

SEX AND INTIMACY ARE NOT SYNONYMOUS

There are numerous reasons why a woman may not enjoy sex with her partner. Dr. Sommers notes, "Inadequate stimulation from one's partner or one's self plays a role, but in my view it is the lack of focused attention which is very important. Some women lack an internal 'permission' within themselves to fully *let go*."

Perhaps you are having regular sex with your husband but don't feel as connected or intimate as you used to feel in bed. Generally speaking, people who behave intimately are able to escape their mental chatter so they can be swept away by the experience that they're sharing with another person. Sometimes the intimacy is expressed through emotions, in which deep thoughts, dreams, fears, or vulnerabilities are shared; sometimes intimacy is expressed physically through loving acts like kissing and cuddling.

It's probably no surprise that the average woman reports feeling turned on following an emotional connection with her partner, or after seeing her partner step up and attend to her needs. For women, the desire for sexual connection often comes from an intimate moment shared outside the bedroom. Perhaps their partners opened up to them, pitched in around the house to help them, or supported them through a personal challenge. Whatever the situation, emotional intimacy is an important component of many women's sexual appetites.

One aspect of intimacy that some women struggle with is the element of relinquishing control of their inner worlds and sharing their feelings and emotions. Of course, when you are consciously communicating with your spouse and feeling connected to him, you will experience more intimacy in your relationship. However, when you're feeling disconnected from your husband and going through the motions in your marriage or in your life, you will not be as inclined to open up and share. The blahs will carry over to the bedroom. But the truth is that in any relationship—and especially in a marriage—you cannot have intimacy without vulnerability.

The physical response of an orgasm is especially difficult to achieve when this level of vulnerability and intimacy isn't present. When you hold back your thoughts and feelings in an attempt to maintain control over your emotions or protect yourself from being hurt, you're also undermining the possibility of achieving true intimacy with your husband.

If you find that you cannot get out of your head, you may consider practicing meditation or deep breathing on a regular basis—any exercise to remind you of the power of staying in the moment. Or you may add a ritual before bedtime, like lighting a candle or taking a bath. Most women cannot connect to their sensuality and turn on intimacy immediately, so experiment with different approaches and see what helps you center your body and quiet your mind.

You are with your husband because he is someone with whom you wanted to build a life, someone who you believed would make your life more meaningful. You signed a marriage contract because you trusted him not only with your assets but with your emotions. You would have stopped dating him if you felt unsafe, insecure, or unsure that he could support you and help you grow. Giving him a window into your fears and hopes, and enlisting his assistance when you need his help, is a beautiful and authentic way to bring intimacy into your home.

SEXPLORATION

One of the greatest things about having a lifelong sexual partner is that you have full license to take risks together in the bedroom. In a monogamous relationship, you can have unprotected sex, experiment with new techniques, explore fantasies, and do just about anything else you both want. Hopefully, you and your husband have a level of trust and comfort that allows you both to introduce adventure without shame or embarrassment.

Another great aspect of being together long term is that you and your husband know every inch of one another's bodies. You are aware of each other's sensitive zones, and as long as you don't get into too much of a routine (e.g., first kiss his ears, then unzip his pants before having missionary sex), familiarity is a positive aspect of sexual monogamy.

On the other hand, some people are stuck in a sexual routine that is *not* working for them. A number of women have told me that their husbands have been touching them or approaching sex with them in ways they haven't enjoyed for years. One woman said, "For some reason, my husband thinks I like rough sex. I wish he'd slow down. I don't want to tell him because it will seem critical . . . but I don't enjoy sex." Instead of telling her husband that she'd prefer a gentler approach, she avoids sex with him altogether.

Here's a simple truth: Men want you to enjoy sex with them. Wish your partner touched you differently? Want to break out of your ho-hum routine? Dr. Betty Dodson recommends a "show, don't tell" approach. Whenever possible, lead your husband's hand to the area you want to be touched and show him what feels good for you. And if his sexual pace is too fast or too aggressive for your liking, try to slow down the pace yourself and be sure to respond when things are working. You can also guide him with your words. Reinforce the things you do enjoy by letting him know: "I love when you _____. Can you do more of that?"

Dr. Kerner suggests keeping communication about your sex life open and creating a "naughty zone" where you and your partner can express your fantasies and desires without being judged. He said, "You must be willing to communicate what you want. Make your requests sexy. Something like, 'Hey, I have this sexy thought about the two of us,' or 'I had a crazy sexy dream about you last night.' This will compel you to think about activities that may help you reach orgasm."

If you feel unsure of how to verbally communicate your sexual fantasies and needs, consider that many resources, books, and DVDs have been designed to help couples convey their sexual desires. There's no reason you should spend the rest of your marriage (and your life!) feeling sexually unsatisfied. One thing that differentiates your relationship with your husband from your relationships with others is your physical intimacy with him. Studies consistently show that when you are not intimate—or when you're not happy with that physical intimacy—your overall relationship is likely to break down.

A woman I spoke with named Karrie said she enjoys a much happier marriage with her current husband than what she had with her ex-husband 8 years ago. She attributed it, in part, to their healthy sexual relationship. Good sex, she said, helps break up a stressful week, creates connection, resolves tension in her relationship, and allows her to get out of her head. All of those factors are invaluable. Karrie finds it sad that many women don't feel sexually fulfilled. After being in a sexless marriage, she is committed to keeping sex an integral part of her relationship today. She and her husband continue to set expectations, make requests, and share desires with each other. "It's such a wonderful and healthy part of my marriage!" she shared. "I don't do it for him. I do it for us . . . . I do it for me."

While we may not be able to transform ourselves into sex-hungry vixens overnight (or ever), there must be something better than having sex for someone else's sake or settling for something less than what makes us feel good.

When life is busy and communication breaks down in our relationships, we may slip into the role of becoming roommates with our spouses, figuring that we can't be bothered to exert the energy to get our sex lives back on track. We all know how easy it is for days and weeks to turn into months without intimacy, just as we know how integral a healthy and happy sex life is to a healthy and happy marriage. But the reason to stay invested in your intimate relationship is not because of the negative consequences that may occur if you don't; rather, the reason to prioritize your sexual connection with your husband is because of all the positive results that intimacy will bring into your life and your relationship. Couples who have sex report more overall relationship satisfaction.

Your sex life with your partner has changed since you were dating him, but there's no reason it can't be as good as—or even better than—it was when you first met and had marathon make-out sessions. At this point, you know yourself better and you know your partner better. Losing a sexy part of yourself, or a sexy part of your relationship that you used to love, is too important to ignore.

At the bachelorette brunch that day, Jenni was one of the few women who said that she loves having sex with her husband. She put it this way: "When I have sex with my husband, I get to transform into an irresistible hot chick, get a little exercise, release some stress, get excited, and be relaxed. Why wouldn't I want that in my life?" Her declaration prompted everyone at the table to clink their glasses and wish the bride-to-be a fabulous sex life with her new husband. Soon after, a few women admitted that they were feeling a little frisky. These women were inspired by hearing Jenni's perspective. They realized that they could feel that way, too, if they wanted to.

CHAPTER NINE

Sweat the Small Stuff

True life is lived when tiny changes occur.
—Leo Tolstoy

Richard Carlson's bestselling book *Don't Sweat the Small Stuff* carried the core message that in life we must pick our battles daily. Carlson's intention was to show his readers that they would feel less stressed if they stopped worrying so much about the minor things that probably won't affect their lives in a major way. When it comes to putting too much attention on everyday nuisances, I agree with Carlson—I believe in choosing your battles and not investing your energy today in worries that won't matter to you tomorrow.

But, in general, I believe small stuff *is* worth sweating. It's the small stuff that teaches you the most about a person, causes you to miss him or her, makes an experience memorable, helps us bond with others, and connect with the vast universe. Haven't you ever witnessed a simple moment in nature and felt connected to something much larger than yourself?

In business, consumers will pay for the details. The first hotel chain to put coffee dispensers in guest rooms saw increased occupancy rates. The first car manufacturer to put cup holders in vehicles saw increased sales. In a 2004 *New*

Yorker article, Malcolm Gladwell examined the surge of sport-utility vehicle purchases and referred to French cultural anthropologist G. Clotaire Rapaille, who stated, "It's amazing that intelligent, educated women will look at a car and the first thing they will look at is how many cup holders it has."

People notice the small stuff.

Whenever I miss someone, I'm always painfully aware of the small stuff. After a breakup with a significant boyfriend, I rarely missed him on big occasions, like Valentine's Day or his birthday; I missed him when I walked by something that reminded me of an inside joke we shared or when I heard a song on the radio that he loved. And I still laugh when I think of the shtick my grandfather used to do when he greeted me ("Andrea, do me favor—go upstairs and see if I'm there . . . ."). I miss the smell of his suit jacket.

In any relationship, the little things you do make far more of an impression than the grand gestures you make. Back when I was dating—and even today when I meet new people—it's the small things they do (or don't do) that help me decide if we're compatible. If someone is rude to a waiter, or judgmental about the things I value most, I realize we are not going to click. It's often as simple—and as little—as that.

In your marriage, the small stuff (and often an accumulation of many small things) is what keeps you feeling connected—or contributes to your feelings of frustration. And yet, when we think about making changes in our marriages, we often frame it in terms of taking giant strides instead of small, deliberate steps—and we get overwhelmed by the challenge.

I spoke with a mother of two who avoids having date nights with her husband because she says she feels too much pressure for the outings to be perfect. She admitted that it's easier to hang out at home with her husband, because then she's not invested in the idea that a night out will completely transform their relationship, allow them to bond deeply, and get their relationship back on a romantic track. I responded, "Who told you that one night out with your husband had to mean all of that?" She was caught in an all-or-nothing trap.

WHY ALL OR NOTHING GENERALLY LEAVES YOU WITH NOTHING

Too often, we put pressure on ourselves to do something perfectly or not do it at all. This reminds me of people who decide to raid the fridge after they indulge in dessert because they've "already cheated" on their healthy diets.

A number of people hold the perspective of all or nothing. When I graduated from broadcast journalism school, a friend asked me, "Will you take this job or that job—or will you forget this industry altogether?" I replied, "Neither. I'll take another job. I'll find, or create, another choice that I'm interested in." The fact that I added a third option baffled her, but it's the reason that I'm in a job I love today.

Think about how many expressions are based on the all-or-nothing model: It's time to fish or cut bait. Do or die. It's either uphill or downhill from here. Feast or famine!

When you look at anything from a black-and-white vantage point, you invest too much in one experience. (Anyway, I've always felt life is best lived in color.) I'm not a fan of extremes— in philosophy or language. Broad statements like *always* or *never* are unrealistic and can often be self-defeating. How can anyone know about the always or nevers that she will encounter before she has lived a full life?

An all-or-nothing approach to life—and marriage—is a recipe for dissatisfaction. While I think it's great to delve into something with extreme dedication and focus, it's important to do so with the knowledge that even if you don't immediately master it, you can learn from the experience and there may be an even better option that hasn't yet occurred to you. When you hold a perspective of abundance, rather than of scarcity, you know that your happiness does not depend on one result or the other and that there are many paths toward fulfillment.

I asked the woman who avoids date nights why 2 hours away from home with her husband has to mean *everything*. She admitted that it's rare that they find time to get away, so the event would carry tremendous significance. I posed two simple questions: "What if the idea of time together was more regular? And instead of big, romantic, pressure-filled evenings, what if you could steal a couple of hours a month to connect uninterrupted and commit to that?" She liked the idea, but I could tell that my challenge didn't feel realistic to her. I reminded her that it's a lot easier to work on the small stuff than to institute major changes. The only commitment she would have to make would be to take a few steps away from her regular routine and to create a new routine that incorporates some of the elements of her relationship that she is missing—the elements that helped her bond with her husband in the first place. They used to be adventurous, romantic, and interesting, she told me. They used to have dynamic conversations. She missed that. I reminded her that those qualities are still in both of them, and even though it's more difficult to express them every single day, they must still find space to express them.

My challenge to her, and to anyone who's married is: What small things can you do in your relationship to shift the dynamic and help you remember why you fell in love with your partner? If you don't like the routine you've fallen into, what's another realistic option you haven't yet considered trying? What's the first step you could take in that direction?

BE PRESENT

There's a joke about a man and woman on a first date, looking over the dinner menu. The man scans it and thinks, "Should I order chicken or fish?" The woman flips through the menu and thinks, "Could I marry this guy? Would my parents like him? What will he be like as a dad?"

When you're spending time alone with your husband, if you're preoccupied with thoughts like "Are we getting along? Are we still attracted? Why aren't we having a great conversation? Was this date night worth all the planning and money?" then you won't be present for the experience of just *being* with him. I often give daters the same advice when they scrutinize their dates: Get out of your head and enjoy the moment!

Many of us have mastered the art of overanalyzing our dates instead of relaxing and enjoying the experience for what it is—an opportunity to connect with someone and perhaps add a little spice or romance to the week.

Being present is a wonderful approach to living happily in your marriage, and in your life, every day. The reason is simple: If you daydream about what was and yearn for the past, you will be disappointed (as you can never have that moment in time again); if you obsess about the future, and about events that are unknown and haven't happened yet, you may feel anxious. Don't mistake me—I believe that it's wonderful to take lessons from the past and share memories that can spark great things for you today. I also know that thinking about the future you are building with your spouse is important to a healthy union. Being inspired by the past and driven for your future are useful tools when you look at your relationship on a megalevel. In your everyday interaction with your partner, however, stay present and notice how much easier things are to navigate. Most of the time, being present is a present!

My friend Lori has two kids, an adoring husband, and a busy career—and she's made a commitment to living in the moment in her relationship. For her, it's been an easy decision to be present, as she realizes it makes her life more enjoyable. "My husband and I have discussed this and decided to live our life together based more on today than on hopes for tomorrow," she explained. "It doesn't mean that we don't save for the future or think realistically about the future. Quite the contrary. What it means is that we try to take the time to appreciate what we have right now in front of us, at this very moment. It is this type of thinking that has given us everything we want out of life. I never thought this way until I met my husband. I always dreamed and lived for the future. In doing so, I missed out on the present."

When you are present and appreciate the small gifts around you, you invite gratitude into your life. You will also feel more optimistic about your relationship when you focus on your current situation instead of on a scenario that has passed or has not yet happened. Next time you feel overwhelmed in your life or your relationship, put your attention back on what you can control. Pay attention to how you feel, what you can do, and what you want. Now.

BE CONSCIOUS

To live is the rarest thing in the world.
Most people exist, that is all.
—Oscar Wilde

I'm sure you have experienced days when you can barely remember your commute to work or how many tasks you've completed on your to-do list. When we're in overdrive, we often turn off our rational and conscious thoughts and switch on a sort of automatic pilot—a function of a part of our brain called the hypothalamus. This instinctual response allows us to keep going to get through the day. When stimulated, the hypothalamus produces a fight-or-flight response that helps us survive extreme stress.

Our brains switch into fight-or-flight mode when we're faced with situations of physical threat (for instance, a stranger follows you down a dark street) and emotional threats (you're about to get fired at work). In some instances, this response creates an adrenaline rush and results in elevated heartbeat and shortness of breath—a panic attack.

It's natural for all of us to experience stress at certain points in our lives; our brains are wired to help us adapt to changing environments and respond to threats to our survival. I'm sure you've heard that few people experience physical pain immediately after being shot. The reason is that when the brain perceives danger, it sends a signal to the body to release the hormone adrenaline; and after that is released, the brain sends another signal to produce the stress hormone cortisol. Cortisol elevates blood pressure and blood sugar in order to help someone in danger escape the precarious situation. But our brains and bodies are not wired to experience prolonged periods of stress. When we go for weeks, months, and years feeling stressed and completely overwhelmed, our physical and mental health suffers. Raised levels of cortisol over long periods cause a weakened immune system and impaired memory (too much cortisol actually kills brain cells). The release of the stress hormone on a regular basis damages us in more ways than we may realize.

Sometimes we are not in complete freak-out mode, but we are operating on another level of consciousness, one in which we are not really aware of our stress or our actions. On my last book tour, I had scheduled so many appearances across the country that I often had no memory of how I got back to my hotel room at night. In college, I used to exist in this semiconscious place when I had a paper due and an exam slated in the same week. When I looked back on my paper the following year, I marveled at the fact that I was able to write something mildly coherent under those conditions.

Living on autopilot may help us get through the day and manage life challenges; however, surviving isn't the same thing as thriving. In fact, existing this way over time can be destructive to our emotional and physical health. Few of us find life meaningful or connections with others very deep when we are just going through the motions and *getting by*. When life is busy and stressful, you and your partner may become so disconnected and distracted that you may not even realize you miss each other until years have gone by.

When Socrates said, "An unexamined life is not worth living," he was referring to the power of consciousness and the effectiveness and meaning of self-reflection. The issue we face when we live *unconsciously* is that we cannot learn or grow from our experiences, so life invariably feels flat and uninspired. If you wake up one day in your marriage and wonder, "Is this really it?" examine yourself: How present are you in your relationship? How consciously have you been living your life? When's the last time you took stock of the small things—good and bad—that affect your everyday happiness? Take ownership over the choices you make and the way you live your life. And if something's broken, resolve to fix it.

PRACTICE GRATITUDE

In the 1990s, Oprah Winfrey inspired women across America to keep a gratitude journal after she suggested that taking the time to bask in appreciation of the small things that entered their lives every day would make them happier.

You may wonder if writing down the things you're grateful for really has any impact on your happiness. Actually, Oprah's suggestion is supported today by real science. Researchers in the field of positive psychology—a relatively recent field of psychology that studies the benefits of positive emotions—have demonstrated that taking the time to count our blessings alleviates stress and enhances our quality of life. In an interview at SharpBrains.com, positive psychology practitioner Dr. Robert Emmons states, "First, the practice of gratitude can increase happiness levels by around 25 percent. Second, this is not hard to achieve—a few hours writing a gratitude journal over three weeks can create an effect that lasts six months if not more. Third, cultivating gratitude brings other health effects, such as longer and better quality sleep time."

Your brain is relatively malleable and capable of change (for years, it was assumed that your brain doesn't change as you age)—a trait scientists refer to neuroplasticity. When you choose to focus your attention on the positive things in your life, you use the neural pathways that process these thoughts and emotions, making them stronger. The idea is that over time you can train your brain to default to a state of positive thinking by reinforcing these "happy" pathways. Consciously focusing our attention on the good things in our lives is beneficial not only for us as individuals, it's also a good exercise to practice in our marriages. Many of us are so focused on what's wrong in our relationships that we don't take the time to consider what's right. When's the last time you thought about the good things your spouse does every day? Consider keeping a gratitude journal and writing down several things each day you're grateful for in your life and your marriage.

Here are a few examples of the things I'm grateful for. It's my "What I love about Michael" list:

○ Thoughtful—with me and everything he touches, even his plants and fish.

○ Passionate—about everything from music to teaching. He rarely does anything if his heart and soul isn't into it.

○ Loyal—he will do anything for his family and makes sure they come first. He often gives me the clothes off his back when I'm cold!

○ Wise—he has amazing intuition about people and events. He can explain something simply that others (read: me) would likely overanalyze.

○ Hilarious—he does the best impressions and puts on silly accents and can transform an otherwise boring afternoon into a playful one.

Remember the effort you used to put forth when you and your partner were dating, and the praise and compliments you exchanged with your then-boyfriend? Even if you played hard to get, you likely focused on your guy's talents in those days and did not take them for granted (or you would not have kept going out with him, after all!). The approval and attention you gave your man are perhaps more important to offer him now, as he is balancing more responsibilities and providing for you and your family (not just physically or financially, but also emotionally and spiritually).

In any relationship, we want to walk away from an interaction leaving someone feeling better, not worse, about ourselves. When we don't get that positive buzz, we generally don't want to continue being in the relationship. (How many of us have ended toxic friendships with girlfriends who brought us down every time we spoke?) We don't want to feel judged or as if we have to walk on eggshells when we speak with someone we care about.

In marriage, it's essential for both parties to feel consistently supported, occasionally adored, and generally comfortable.

Gratitude is one of the simplest and most effective tools for reconnecting with your husband and focusing on the parts of your marriage that you love and appreciate. For couples who are having trouble seeing the positive qualities in their marriage, I recommend trying an exercise called the gratitude diet.

The Gratitude Diet

Tell your husband you would like to try a gratitude experiment: For 30 days, you're going to let him know at least once a day about a small thing he did that impressed you or that you appreciated. Invite him to participate in your gratitude game if he's interested, but there are no strings attached to compliments. Chances are, as the receiver of your gratitude, he will be inspired to start putting positive attention on you as well. You can tell your spouse that it's a social experiment (otherwise, he may think someone slipped something in your drink), but assure him that you're not going to share any gratitude unless you truly believe it.

In Chapter 4, I discussed psychologist Dr. John Gottman's "five to one" rule: Your partner needs to hear five compliments to negate every insult or criticism you express. When you argue, you should not complain with details about your mate's character. (Instead of saying, "You're so lazy and unthoughtful—you don't help with the dishes!" it's better to say, "I'd appreciate it if you helped with the dishes.") However, the opposite is true with positive feedback: Reference your partner's positive characteristics with a few specifics. Putting the attention on aspects of his personality and character that you appreciate will produce a more positive interaction. For instance, you may randomly tell your husband that you appreciate how thoughtful he is whenever he gives you an extra hour to sleep while he takes care of the kids, or how talented you think he is at work and why you think he stands out.

Reinforcing his character traits, positive behavior, and the small things he does that you admire will make him feel appreciated and as a bonus—will likely make him want to please you more!

CHORE PLAY

There are no great acts, only small acts done with great love.
—Mother Teresa

Much of the way we communicate is nonverbal: through our gestures, body language, and actions. You and your husband both need verbal reinforcement of your appreciation for one another as well as physical demonstrations of your love.

In most marriages, each partner has a basic idea of the domestic tasks that he or she is responsible for to keep the home in order. Some couples clearly delineate these tasks when they first move in together; others let the assignation of domestic duties happen more organically. In general, couples don't discuss this division of labor unless something is out of balance. If one person feels that he or she is pulling more than his or her fair share of the weight, arguments tend to spring up.

In our home, Michael and I each have an idea, more or less, of our domestic roles. For instance, I buy and prepare the food. Michael disposes of the food (i.e., he eats most of it . . . and takes out the trash). Michael tends to wash the dishes, and I dry them. Michael decorates and builds furniture for our home, and I . . . don't.

Having a clear division of domestic tasks can be helpful, but it shouldn't stop you from veering away from your usual role every now and then. In fact, chore play may be one of the most underrated and easiest ways to seduce your partner in marriage!

Case in point: My friend Steve's partner, Dan, does most of the cooking in their home because he is an amazing chef and a culinary school graduate. Recently, Steve could tell that Dan had had a stressful day at work, and he decided to give Dan some time to relax by picking up dinner duty. When Dan came downstairs, he was touched and surprised to find that Steve had taken the initiative to prepare the meal. The sight of Steve putting something in the oven warmed Dan's heart, and the two shared an unexpected romantic evening.

Steve explained how such a small thing shifted the dynamic in their relationship. "It gave me a lot of pleasure to help him out before he even had a chance to ask," he said. "And the look on his face told me he was surprised and really appreciated the gesture."

In marriage, sometimes the smallest things can have the biggest impact. If your husband warms up your car on a cold day, or if you get up first to make the coffee and you bring him a mug in bed, you are engaging in *chore play*. When you are busy and stressed, what's more seductive and thoughtful than a small gesture to make your day a little easier?

When I told my friend Lori about my "sweat the small stuff" philosophy, she enthusiastically agreed that the details are important in her marriage. I received an e-mail from her later that night that expressed how essential the small things are to her and her family. "My entire relationship with my husband is based on doing small things for each other," she wrote. "With two little children, and both of us working from home, there isn't much wiggle room for big nights on the town, European vacations, or the kinds of things and the adventures we used to do when we were dating. So it's the small (to some, mundane) things that keep our relationship going. For example, when it comes to the household chores, one person cooks and the other does the dishes; one of us goes grocery shopping and the other brings it in from the car and puts it all away. These are only two examples, but they are the foundation for our household. One of the sweetest things that my husband does for me, without me ever asking, is letting me sleep in when he knows I'm exhausted. He quietly takes care of our 3-month-old and 2-year-old and makes sure they don't disturb me until I wake up. This recharges me for days."

I asked Lori what small stuff she does for her husband. She said, "I surprise him with his favorite cooked meal, buy his favorite foods, or fill the gas tank of his car even when it's not completely empty (especially if I know he'll be traveling the next day). It's the everyday things that bring us together as a team, make our life easier, and keep us appreciating each another year after year."

My mom told me that one of the greatest love stories she ever witnessed was the one between her great-aunt Eva and Eva's husband, Harry, who often demonstrated their love through small exchanges. When Harry was in his nineties, very ill and in a hospital bed in their home, his only request was for his wife to sit beside his bed and rub his leg. This simple gesture was something the two had shared for years before Harry was sick, and something that he and his wife were able to continue to do

HONEY, I'M HOME

Greet each other at the door with a kiss every night when you reunite after a day's work and spend a few minutes saying hello. It's okay to spend time and space apart unwinding after that, but greeting each other when you walk in will set the tone and help you feel connected for the rest of the evening.

together when they could no longer communicate in any other way. Harry was weak, inaudible, and immobile in the hospital bed, but my mom remembers how intimate the ritual was between them: "There was a physical and emotional connection, even when he could barely do anything. Eva rubbed his leg every single day. To someone else, it may not have seemed like a big deal—but Eva knew it was a powerful way that she stayed connected to her husband and nurtured him." Intimacy certainly comes in many forms.

DON'T SWEAT *ALL* THE SMALL STUFF

I know Michael hates the way I dry the dishes, and I don't like how cranky he is when he's tired, but we have learned to adapt instead of argue. There are bigger issues for us to disagree about, so I'd rather not waste time on these annoyances!

Cara Raich and Esther Rosenfeld, who are family mediators, both mentioned that one issue many of their clients have in common is difficulty picking their battles in their relationships. When communication breaks down, resentments build up, and every little thing can set off a fight. The issue, of course, is that if you constantly fight over (ostensibly) small things, the tiff is usually a symptom of a larger problem or pattern. It's essential to recognize this theme, if it is one that resonates with you, so that you and your partner can tackle the real issues behind the small battles.

One couple I know argue over using too much water when washing the dishes. The husband consistently complains that his wife isn't mindful of her water consumption, and the wife complains to friends that she is using a normal amount of water and her husband is uptight. The issue behind the water fight is the husband's passion about environmental issues and water conservation. He likely feels that his value is being stepped on each time his partner leaves the water running when he perceives she does not need it. To him, this is not a small issue, because it affects his core beliefs and values.

When battling any topic with your partner, ask yourself: How will this affect me tomorrow? In a week? In a month? In a year? Break your query into bite-size pieces. It may be helpful to look at the big picture so you don't get caught up in arguing over something that won't matter in the long term. If you discover, however, that your issue is one that *will* affect you and potentially damage your relationship over time, commit to working through it together rather than avoiding it or recycling the same complaints. Ostensibly small issues may carry more weight and significance to your partner. Take the time to find out.

As we discussed in Chapter 4, most couples tend to act out the same conflicts and replay the same arguments for years—that's normal. However, if you find you are complaining about your partner more than you are enjoying being around him, or if you find you are getting into major fights over small things, it may be time to examine the larger issues at play in your marriage and commit to working through them with open communication and/or a mediator or a counselor. Constantly complaining about an issue like organization in the home is often a signal that someone is defending his or her value of being orderly. Focus on the real issue, the value behind the complaint, instead of getting caught up in the minutiae.

SURVIVAL OF THE FITTEST WIFE

(I'm not talking about the size of your jeans.)

Survival of the fittest in marriage today requires resilience, yes, but it also requires resourcefulness and adaptability to our ever-changing environment. These skills are essential in many aspects of life and certainly are more important to your marriage than any textbook definition of being a perfect wife.

If you are prone to worry easily, stress over things you can't control, or don't adapt well to change, you will not only *not* be productive in those scenarios, you will be counterproductive. You simply can't be in control of everything your partner does or plan for everything that transpires in your household. The Dalai Lama once said, "If you have fear of some pain or suffering, you should examine whether there is anything you can do about it. If you can, there is no need to worry about it; if you cannot do anything, then there is also no need to worry."

One of my favorite mantras is "I'm stressed about this *and* I'm going to get through it." You can acknowledge your feelings and not be defeated by them or by things you cannot control.

Committing to stay present, become more aware (so that you are not operating on the autowife or automom function), and embrace a perspective that values and honors the small stuff will help you navigate difficult situations and create new, exciting possibilities in your marriage. After all, it is the small gestures you and your husband do for each other, and the small moments between you, that build intimacy and reaffirm your connection. It is the small things, like rubbing Harry's leg, that his wife missed when he died.

When we are able to break down the small steps, instead of trying to wrap our brains and schedules around the giant leaps, we are more likely to honor and attend to our relationships.

So—what will be your first step?

CHAPTER TEN

Be the Partner You Want to Have

If we are together nothing is impossible. If we are divided all will fail.
—Winston Churchill

FRIENDSHIP ISN'T ENOUGH

I've often heard singles say that they're looking for a "best friend" to spend the rest of their lives with. A woman in one of my dating workshops declared, "I've had enough of jerks—I want a friend to marry! That's all I'm looking for." I asked her, "Really? That's *all* you need in a husband?"

I understood her sentiment—she wanted to find a great guy to spend her life with who would always be there for her, championing her toward success and supporting her in tough times. But I didn't think she really meant that she wanted to find a friend to marry (or she might have already married one of the 217 male friends on her Facebook page). We both knew there were other qualities that her life partner would have to offer, in addition to his friendship.

What distinguishes your husband from your male friends is that he is your lover, your companion (there to physically participate in life's events with you, not just to emotionally support you as a friend), and your partner. His friendship may be one of the qualities you appreciate most about your marriage, but it is not the only ingredient of a successful union. Presumably you have other good friends in your life, so it's not a unique role for your spouse to offer. Friendship is necessary but not a sufficient criterion in a marriage. Other criteria, like whether or not your spouse is your lover and a good partner, are integral and critical parts of a healthy marriage.

THERE'S A DIFFERENCE BETWEEN BEING A GOOD PERSON AND BEING A GOOD PARTNER

When we are single, we often spend a lot of time focused on the qualities we are looking to find in a person, while we should be focusing most of our attention on the characteristics we require in a *partner*. Partnership is inextricably linked to marriage; without someone who is a good partner, you're likely to feel very alone and unsupported.

A partner is someone who is aligned with your values and appreciates the meaning of compromise. When you are someone's partner, you realize that your own happiness is directly tied to your partner's happiness. You will do whatever it takes to get your relationship to a place of mutual respect and understanding because you know that the ultimate goal of marriage is for two people—not just one—to be happy and fulfilled.

We all do things for our spouses that we may not want to do, but we make our choices based on what's best for our partnerships. Anytime you take care of your spouse when he's sick, support him through a tough time at work, or help your in-laws, you are stepping up as your husband's partner and showing him you're on the same team. In everyday life, the small things like attending one of his work events or choosing a restaurant you know he loves are other examples of how you demonstrate your commitment to being his partner.

I recently witnessed successful partnership in action when I visited a friend over the holidays. My friend and her husband were dealing with in-law stresses and cranky kids. Through the chaos, they organized everything in a way that comes only from a conscious "we're in it together" attitude and from years of navigating situations as partners. My friend placated her mother while her husband took the kids to another room for a time out. Neither partner seemed to be pulling all the weight that afternoon, and they were able to laugh about the stress (which they jokingly referred to as "the holiday spirit") and reflect on it over brunch the next morning. Imagine the same situation, but with one partner focused on his or her own comfort and needs rather than coming from a perspective of partnership. When you don't support each other and focus on the same goals, even a slightly stressful morning can turn into a situation that doesn't benefit anyone.

BE THE PARTNER YOU WANT TO HAVE

One important aspect of partnership is realizing that you are *not* one being (sorry, Jerry Maguire); both of you have individual needs and perspectives.

I've worked with women who complain that their partners don't treat them as they want to be treated—but acknowledge that they don't act the way they want to be treated. One woman in a workshop I taught told me that she wanted to be admired, adored, and always treated with kindness by her husband. She was frustrated that he no longer talked to her as he had when they were dating. She laughed nervously when I asked if she consistently offers those qualities to her spouse.

I spoke with my friend Vanessa, who admitted that she hates how she fights with her husband. She said that he remains calm and rational, whereas she becomes childish, raising her voice and storming out of the room before they can discuss the issue. She said, "Recently, my husband told me, 'I'm not you. Accept it or don't.' "He didn't want to fight with her, he just wanted her to understand that they had different points of view and different ways of handling the situation—and he wanted his voice to be heard and considered. It was a poignant moment for Vanessa, who realized that she didn't want to be married to herself and that she wasn't giving her husband's perspective enough thought.

"I would love to fight more fairly," Vanessa admitted. "I want to be the partner to him that he is to me. Marriage is a mirror to my flaws. Sometimes my husband says something and I realize what a jerk I'm being."

For Vanessa, being reminded that her needs and her voice are not the only considerations is one of the most powerful parts of partnership. Having that "marriage mirror" is why she feels she has grown as an individual since she's been with her spouse.

Think about the qualities you want your husband to have. Perhaps you wish he were more compassionate, patient, or successful. Whatever you want in him reflects your values and may be something you need to work on yourself. You can't rely on your spouse to meet all of your needs. How do you cultivate those qualities in your own life?

A HAPPY WIFE MAKES A HAPPY LIFE

How many times have you been to a wedding and heard a groomsman make a toast that includes the saying, "A happy wife makes a happy life"? I hear it so often that I'm starting to think it must be part of a secret top-10 wedding speeches collection.

Of course, your husband should be considerate and thoughtful about your feelings and needs; after all, that is one of the ways he shows up as your partner. Ultimately, though, your happiness in life is in your own hands. You are not a passenger in your life or in your marriage. You are driving the relationship, as much as your husband is, to ensure that it is moving forward—and that each of you is moving forward as an individual.

You have to embrace the idea of being a happy wife as much as he does.

Raquel, who says she hasn't felt like herself since becoming a mother a couple of years ago, remarked, "A marriage can only be as happy as the partners are with themselves. A relationship will be half-happy if only one person is happy. I want to be a good example to our daughter. I owe it to her to be the best and most complete woman I can be."

Cynthia, a fellow life coach, said she was very frustrated with her partner recently and realized that she was asking him to give her something she needed to give herself. According to Cynthia, "Giving ourselves what we need makes our relationships so much easier."

Her turning point occurred one night when she and her spouse were having a fight because Cynthia was having a tough day and felt like her husband wasn't supporting her emotionally. "I crossed an invisible line that neither of us saw," she reflected. "We both tripped. He shut down and walked away, and I retreated to the bedroom. Pouting, maybe . . . ranting, definitely. Why couldn't he just hug me, hold me, smile at me?" And then, something clicked and Cynthia realized she shouldn't blame her husband for her sad mood that day—it probably had nothing to do with him, anyway. She decided to change her approach and put the focus back on what she could control, not what she wished her husband would do. That perspective allowed her to break her usual fighting pattern (one in which she gets emotional and her husband calms her down).

"I looked in the mirror and thought, wouldn't life be so much easier if I just give myself what I need, rather than sitting here as the victim? Waiting for some vague need to be met? One I can't even clearly identify? I had a talk with myself. What is it I need, right now, right this moment?"

The answer came to her moments later. "I needed to give myself a hug," Cynthia recalled. "Sounds silly, but I did it. I told myself I was doing just fine. I had a lot on my plate and should give myself a break. I told myself what I needed to hear and feel. It's crazy, but the hug felt good. The conversation I had with myself was meaningful and hit home, and it released my husband from having to read my mind, meet my needs, find a way to make me feel better. It wasn't his job, it was my job."

How did you take care of yourself when you didn't have your partner to fix things? How did you handle bad days when you were single? You may have called your friends Ben and Jerry to help you cope during those times, but presumably you also reached out to girlfriends and family for support and accessed your own inner strength for comfort. When you are stuck waiting for your husband to meet a need that you may need to meet yourself, reconnect with the woman who was resilient and resourceful. She's still in you.

KING AND QUEEN FOR A DAY

Imagine you wake up on a Saturday morning and your husband announces that you're Queen for a Day. He won't let you race anywhere to do one of your many errands—he will do what he can do for you. He tells you that he doesn't want you to lift a finger and that your wish is his command. If you have children, he's assured you that he already made arrangements for them to play with friends. If you want to spend the day with them or with him, he can accommodate your request.

I've posed this scenario to a number of women. Some have exclaimed, "Sign me up!" but a fair number said not being in control of the day's activities and the family's plans would make them uncomfortable. When I've probed and asked why they wouldn't want to be treated all day, some admitted that they're so used to taking care of everything and everyone that it would be hard to give up that role, and they wouldn't be able to relax (of course, herein lies the issue and the point of the exercise!). Interestingly, when I've posed this scenario to men, most have found the idea of being King for a Day very appealing.

I know someone who did this exercise with her spouse for the first time 4 years ago and has since decided to institute King and Queen for a Day biannually. She says it works wonders for a relationship.

"Last time I granted my husband the title King Robert, he decided to watch sports in his boxers and eat wings and drink beer." (Not very regal, I noted, though I'm sure he felt good.) "At night, he wanted to do something for me, and I had to remind him that those weren't the rules!"

What does she order her husband to do when she is Queen for a Day? She joked that most of the time she likes him to do her boring errands like pick up the dry cleaning, clean the bathroom, or drop the kids off at one of their lessons or a friend's house. Occasionally, she'll ask for a foot massage.

"It's not so much what the activities are that makes this exercise fun," she said. "I think it's great because my husband and I are putting aside time to make the other person feel special without expecting anything in return. So many of those things each of us would love to do get buried when we're busy, and this forces us to stop and take a moment to love and treat each other again."

Let your partner set the tone for the day or the night, down to where you will dine and what you'll wear. Allow yourself to relax and trust that your husband can manage you and the household for one day, without your assistance. How does it feel to surrender control? Then, on another date, plan a day around your partner's wants. Notice how the dynamic of your partnership shifts when you allow your partner to be put on a (temporary) pedestal and get completely pampered. Notice how you feel when you let go of your routine and responsibilities.

Giving your spouse (or yourself) a full day to reconnect with the person you are outside your roles and obligations in marriage is a precious gift—one that allows you to remember how great it feels to make someone you love feel good and reminds you that sometimes your husband can carry the weight—if you give him the chance.

A true partnership is one in which both people are mindful of the other's needs and work together to create a happier and healthier relationship. The great thing about partnership is that the more you show up as a partner, the more your partner will be inspired to do the same.

Earlier, I mentioned Dave and Dolores, who have been married for close to 40 years. One of the reasons they say their marriage has survived (and thrived!) is because they enjoy doing things for the other person and know that their relationship isn't a 50/50 effort. Rather, they are both committed to putting in 100 percent of themselves. When you do things for your spouse to make his life a little easier, he is less likely to feel as if he is lacking attention, time, or resources.

Anticipating your partner's needs is an aspect of long-term partnership, but how do you know what your spouse really needs or wants? When was the last time you asked him?

THE INTERVIEW

Some of us daydream about what life used to be like before marriage or parenthood, or what we would like to have that is missing in our relationships, but we do not discuss these topics with our spouses because of loyalty or fear of offending them or being misunderstood. Having a frank discussion with your partner about his needs and wants, and about what he is missing in his life, may seem like a difficult topic to broach, but engaging in this kind of open conversation will build intimacy and allow each of you to understand the other a little more. It will also spark curiosity and learning, which is one of the best ways to curb boredom in your relationship.

Consider clearing time and space one day this month for you and your spouse to interview one another. Write down your questions in advance (though going off-script is encouraged). You might ask him questions like "Who were you before we met? What parts of yourself or your old life do you feel that you've lost? What do you miss about the connection we had when we were dating? Is there anything you miss about me?"

Each of you should try to be present and really hear one another's answers without interjecting your own opinions. This means that while your partner is sharing his perspective, you have to reserve your judgment or your defenses and allow him to open up. He may acknowledge that he prefers where he is with you today to where you were together when you were dating; or he may admit something difficult to hear—that he misses how you related to each other years ago, how you used to act, or some of the freedoms that he had in his life before he settled down. His feedback will provide valuable insight for both of you to continue to grow as partners and to honor each other.

I worked with a couple as they completed this exercise. They've been married for 7 years and have a 3-year-old daughter. The husband admitted that he missed going out and seeing his friends. His wife was not defensive when she heard this; in fact, she told him she wished he had spoken up sooner or had taken the initiative to plan time out with his friends, without feeling like he needed to have her permission. She told him, "If you plan it in advance and tell me, I'd be happy for you to have time to bond with your buddies." He acknowledged that he felt guilty leaving her out. For that reason, he has held back. She responded, "Go, go, go! Have a boys' night and I'll have a girls' night at home with our daughter."

As the interview continued, the husband also admitted that he missed how sensual his wife was when they were dating. Since the rules of the interview were not to interrupt, his wife listened to him as he explained that he still found her beautiful and sexy but wished she embodied her femininity as she used to. Instead of reacting defensively, as she would have previously done (reminding him that it's not easy to be sexy with a toddler hanging off her), she listened to his feedback and agreed that it was something she missed, too.

When it was the wife's turn to share her responses, she admitted that she missed the effort her husband used to put forth to romance her. He used to draw her baths and compliment her regularly. She agreed with her husband that their relationship had gotten better over time but also agreed that she missed how he used to be with her. He used to take initiative; now if they have a date night, it's up to her to arrange the logistics. He acknowledged her position.

After they completed the exercise, the husband planned a night out with his college friends. Then he scheduled a date to a beautiful winery in the area where he and his wife went during their courtship. The couple followed up to let me know that this simple tweak has been great for their relationship. He feels lucky to have a supportive partner, he told me, and she is thankful to have a receptive husband.

Life changes after we get married and start a family, but we should still be able to recognize ourselves. As partners, we can help each other get there.

IF YOU DON'T GROW TOGETHER, YOU'LL GROW APART

Even after you and your husband have a candid conversation, it's important to recognize that both of your wants and needs may look different next year. You, your partner, and your partnership will change and grow over the years. Be sure to keep communication at the forefront of your marriage if you want to grow in the same direction.

Many of my clients begin their sentences with the words "My husband never . . . ." When you say the *never* word in a relationship, it's self-defeating. You negate the possibility that your partner may grow or surprise you (or himself) and that your expectations of what you need from him may change as well. While it's true that people's core values stay more or less consistent throughout the years, research shows that peoples' preferences and tastes change over time and experience.

A recent study conducted by University of Basel psychologists Benjamin Scheibehenne and Jutta Mata was cited in a 2010 *Wired* article, "Love Makes You Increasingly Ignorant of Your Partner." The research demonstrated that young couples are better able to accurately predict their partners' food, movie, and design preferences than are their older counterparts. Those who had been married for decades and who were between the ages of 62 and 78 were more likely to make inaccurate assumptions about their partners' taste.

There are many reasons for this discrepancy, including the fact that couples who have been married for longer periods perceive themselves and their partners as becoming more alike over time and therefore make assumptions about their interests. Our tastes change over the years, but those in long partnerships may no longer openly discuss one another's preferences as they once did.

A few months before I got married, I interviewed an elderly man for an article. When he asked me about how I was feeling about my upcoming marriage, I confidently declared, "I know Michael really well, since we were friends first. I know all his hot buttons!" I continued to make predictions about our future as husband and wife. The man interrupted me and said plainly, "How can you know everything about Michael when he doesn't even know everything about himself? How can you know how you'll feel or what you will do in the relationship when life changes? You don't know."

He proceeded to wish me well and offer us his blessing. It was a bizarre blessing, but one that stuck with me. It was honest, it was based on experience (he had been married for more than 50 years), and it was a reality check. His message—that I didn't know everything about my husband and should be prepared for things to keep changing—was both disconcerting and exciting.

We make assumptions based on what our partners do and don't or won't do, and we turn these assumptions into facts. Anytime I decide or assume that Michael won't like something that I want to try, I may be missing out on an opportunity for us to share a new experience. Of course, there are certain constants, like the fact that my husband hates small talk and therefore dislikes many of the events I attend for work. I don't expect him to transform into a Chatty Cathy at my next media mixer, but there have been times I haven't invited him to a party or asked him to join me in something I wanted to try with him because I decided—without asking him—that it wasn't in his best interest. Michael didn't invite me camping last summer, figuring I wouldn't be comfortable sleeping under the stars. I was surprised by his assumption, since I thought he knew that nights in the woods at camp were some of my favorite summertime activities as a child. I love bonfires, making s'mores, and looking at the stars (especially since, in the city, the only stars I see are the ones in the movies). I love camping.

Making projections about your partner is a surefire way to cut off excitement and the element of surprise in your marriage.

While it's normal to get accustomed to certain roles in your relationship (e.g., one of you is the disciplinarian and the other is the diplomat, or one of you is the talker and the other is the listener), try to leave some space for one another to evolve. If you don't acknowledge that you are both people who continue to grow over time, you may not ever venture outside your respective comfort zones.

The moment you stop being curious and open about your partner or your partnership's evolution, your marriage will start to stagnate—and you may one day find yourself with a case of the blahs. Marriage isn't about coexisting with someone else. It's about creating and growing through life together. Partnerships should be grounded (I'm not a fan of nonstop relationship drama) *and* dynamic. It's human nature, perhaps, to crave stability and variety, but in partnership, these elements are not mutually exclusive.

DREAM TOGETHER

One way to keep your partnership moving forward, and to reignite the excitement you had when dating, is to share common goals. Whether it's an adventurous goal to climb Machu Picchu or a financial goal to build a business together, it is essential to dream with your partner to stay connected and inspired in your marriage.

Your aspirations may be big, but the steps you take toward them can be small. If you've always wanted to travel to Spain, you don't have to book a trip to Madrid. You can start moving toward your dream by enrolling in a Spanish cooking class and in language lessons with your husband. Or contribute to a monthly paella fund. Working together on behalf of a shared goal, and enjoying the process as you move toward it, strengthens your partnership.

Esther, who has been with her husband for 6 years, says that dreaming of their future together is a staple of their relationship. She and her partner discuss their individual goals and the things they want to experience together in the years ahead. "A key component of our marriage is our desire to always improve, build on, and discover our next adventure," Esther remarked. "We have dreams for retirement and fantasize about it, but we also discuss our shorter-term dreams. We always seem to have a trip planned that we can look forward to. Traveling is great because you don't just have the week away to enjoy together. You prepare for it before you leave and reflect on it when you are back. Some of my best memories with my husband are from our shared adventures."

Cynthia and her husband, Gerald, believe that discussing their common ground and shared goals keeps their relationship meaningful and (healthily) unpredictable. Each year during the holidays and before the New Year, she and Gerald work on separate dream lists and vision boards and regroup to compare notes. They have ritualized the process and say it is something they look forward to, as a couple, every year.

Reflecting on this annual tradition, Cynthia said, "We find that so many of our dreams and visions are the same and include each other. But we also have ones that are separate—like his love of singing and drumming. That's not my thing, but he has identified it as important to him, so it's important to me. I love to hear him sing and drum down in our basement. I know when he's doing that, he is a happier, more passionate person for me. Do I love hearing drums echo through the house? From anyone else, no. From Gerald, yes. Because when he drums, I hear his passion, not the music."

It seems logical for a partner to encourage a spouse's personal expression, though Cynthia acknowledges that she knows couples who feel insecure or threatened by their partners' passions. She feels lucky that she and her husband encourage one another to cultivate interests and believes it is one of the reasons they have a healthy marriage. She said, "When I want to go to yet another photography class, my husband says GO! He knows when that passion is fed, his job as my husband is much easier."

As the parents of five, three of whom live with them at home, Cynthia and Gerald love working together on goals as a family and also feel that it is essential to put in the effort to check in with each other as husband and wife. Cynthia is aware that even without children, couples can lose sight of their shared dreams. She said, "Creating our dream lists and vision boards shows us not only where we want to go but how far we have come. It's great to enjoy how working together has accomplished things over the past year, to pat ourselves on the back and give a symbolic high five. It binds us together to know we are creating our lives together. At the end of each year, we book a special dinner out. We recap our year and talk about what we are going to change, do, create in the next year. I love that ritual. It is one of our highlights."

HELP YOUR PARTNER BECOME A BETTER PERSON

An aspect of modern partnership is recognizing that you don't have to adhere to arbitrary or antiquated ideas about what it means to be a perfect wife or a good husband—we can each define what we need from our spouses based on what's right for our lives. Today, most of us in a relationship want to be seen and celebrated for who we are and challenged to be even better.

When I was a self-proclaimed (and let's face it, mass-proclaimed by some of my ex-boyfriends) commitment-phobe who was petrified of marriage, it was because I could not imagine *settling* down and shrinking myself to become one with my partner. In contrast, getting married has had the opposite effect: I have expanded and grown as the result of my partnership.

Psychologists Dr. Art Aron and Dr. Gary W. Lewandowski Jr. assert that the couples who are happiest in their marriages are those who have embraced "self-expansion." According to Dr. Aron, "The self-expansion model assumes that individuals ultimately form relationships to facilitate growth and progress." A key aspect of the self-expansion model is that humans have an innate desire to grow and develop, and a romantic relationship can fulfill this yearning. Their research shows that the more each spouse believes that he or she has grown as an individual because of his or her partner, the more connected and committed the person will feel in the marriage.

When we're falling in love, our need to grow is fulfilled because the experience is new; however, once we acclimate to our partnership, we have to seek out opportunities to keep being stimulated by novelty and to keep learning.

In a sense, when you are with a loving partner, you not only embody qualities he or she has, you are more likely to develop your own unique attributes (in part, by learning about what your partner values). The self-expansion theory supports my definition of "soul mate" (two people bringing each other to their highest potential) and my belief that when you are with a good partner, you become an even better version of yourself.

Duncan, who has been married to Martine for 5 years, says that partnership has only made him more himself. He noted, "I'm still doing the things I loved to do when I was single, and don't feel I've had to give up any part of myself to be with Martine, but now I have somebody there to support me in what I'm doing and someone who I want to make happy as well. It's not difficult to be supportive, because we respect each other. I can confidently say that my life with my wife is better than my life was when I was single and we were apart." And my friends Lahna and Ralphie admit that their comedy careers took off once they merged lives as partners. They each took professional risks that they may not have pursued had they not challenged one another to strive to book bigger shows, had they not offered each other encouragement and support. They each believe that they became better versions of themselves professionally and personally, in large part due to their relationship. According to Drs. Aron and Lewandowski, the more couples have experienced self-expansion, the more satisfied they are in their relationships.

Vanessa, who is trying to learn how to fight better and more fairly with her husband, says she feels consistently fulfilled in her marriage and is more self-aware than she was before she met her husband. "Be everything that's good in your partner and learn from him. There's always something you will learn from your husband and something he will learn from you. There's learning in partnership."

Have you helped your partner become a better person? Has he helped you grow? To measure how couples have embraced self-expansion in their relationships, associate psychology professor Gary W. Lewandowski Jr., who also runs www.ScienceOfRelationships.com, developed the Sustainable Marriage Quiz. I've listed a few of the questions from the quiz below. Here were the instructions for couples:

Using the following scale, rate your answer to each question according to the way you feel. Answers range from 1 (not very much) to 7 (very much). Then add up your scores and check the scale below to see how your own relationship ranks.

Not Very Much Very Much 1 2 3 4 5 6 7	
How much does being with your partner result in your having new experiences?	
How much does your partner help to expand your sense of the kind of person you are?	
How much do your partner's strengths as a person (skills, abilities, etc.) compensate for some of your own weaknesses as a person?	
How much has being with your partner resulted in your learning new things?	
How much has knowing your partner made you a better person?	
Scores	

30 and above—Highly Expansive. You are gaining a lot of new experiences and reaching new goals as a result of your relationship. Chances are you have a happier, more sustainable relationship as a result.

20 to 29—Moderately Exciting. Your relationship has led to moderate improvements in your life and some new experiences. But there's definitely room for improvement.

Below 20—Low Connection. Your relationship is not creating opportunities that help expand your knowledge and make you feel better about yourself. Make an effort to share new experiences with your partner to improve your relationship.

For personal use only. For educational/research use, please contact Gary W. Lewandowski Jr., PhD, Monmouth University.

THE STEPS FOR SUCCESSFUL PARTNERSHIP

It would be naive to say that the partnership dance is an easy one. It's difficult enough to navigate our own needs and wants as we move through life, much less to try to anticipate or adapt to someone else's preferences and goals. However, when we work as a team with our spouses and try to be the partners we would want to have, the steps become easier (and we don't easily bruise or become discouraged when we step on each other's toes).

In the courtship dance, we are trying to impress each other. In the partnership dance, we rely on each other. As partners, we can help one another realize our potential as individuals and recognize what we can create together as a team. This is one of the great legacies of a healthy and committed partnership, and one that will carry our relationships forward.

CONCLUSION

What's Next?

A number of women I know are talented achievers. They are
smart, passionate, and impressive in their abilities. They
are good mothers, loyal friends, and dedicated employees.
Somehow, though, taking care of their own needs and
prioritizing their husbands and marriages aren't always included
in their definitions of what it means to live successfully. These
women seem to excel at everything but their marriages—the
dream they invested in when they decided to share their lives
with another person and build a family.

Imagine if when you exchanged vows with your husband,
you and he included a promise to let days or weeks pass without
giving each other much attention, or you signed up for a series
of hurtful exchanges with him, in which both of you were left
feeling more frustrated. Or, perhaps worse, you agreed to a lifetime of disconnection and indifference in your marriage. Would
you have danced as happily as you did on your wedding day?

Even those of us who consider ourselves happily married still
need to put in work to embody the commitment we made to
ourselves and our husbands—and that's no small feat. It is easy
to become complacent not just in our marriages, but in our
lives. In fact, being complacent is the easiest option.

Those who are risk averse and who cling to the status quo
(even when it's not working) feel that they don't want to dis-
rupt their lives and rock the boat—so, instead, they dock the

189

boat! They become stagnant in their marriages and in their lives. They don't evolve or grow. They hold on to the perspective that *good enough* is good enough, even when they become victimized by the lack of balance in their lives or bored by their realities.

I spoke with Mindy, who is a mother of three kids under 10. She admits to living on cruise control. "I'm not ready to do a complete transformation. I'm lucky if I just get through the day with my usual load," she said when we discussed the challenge of adding more fun and connection in her marriage and her life. She works through her routine each day as if it's a job she must accept, with few benefits. She's a mommy zombie. She's forgotten that she has a *choice* in the matter of how to live her life, and that she can create the change that would produce better and more positive results.

Creating change in marriage to reignite your partnership does not require embracing a complete lifestyle makeover, but it does demand the commitment to take new actions and possibly adopt a new attitude. Action alone is ineffective long term if it's not driven by an innate desire to move.

To strengthen your partnership, you must adopt a philosophy of curiosity, excitement about the future, and desire to keep working on being the best partner—and person—you can be. You must commit to being (thinking differently about being a wife and woman) *and* doing (taking new steps to breathe vitality into your marriage and your life). It is essential to create momentum in your relationship so that you once again embrace the positive Ps—possibility, potential, and pursuit—that you experienced when you first started dating your husband, and so that you still look forward to getting to know him.

Sweating the small stuff; consistently showing up physically and emotionally in your marriage; communicating by making requests instead of demands; and putting a conscious, meaningful, and fun action plan into place will push your relationship into a more dynamic direction. It is here that you will not only enjoy the merits of a fulfilling marriage but also make great discoveries about yourself.

A key component of maintaining a happy life (not to mention a healthy brain) is a commitment to keep learning. The moment you do not think that your husband or marriage can teach you great lessons, or inspire you to do and be better, may be the moment you check out. Think about your greatest personal or professional accomplishments. Were you proactive in landing your goals or reactive in achieving them? Did your accomplishments land in your lap with little or no effort or energy asserted on your part? Why should aligning with your goals in your relationship be any different?

Raquel, who wonders if her experience in her marriage is *normal,* realizes she needs to wake up her own desire if she wants to continue enjoying her relationship. She admits that she's sick of coasting through life. She said, "I think of the expression that says if you're coasting, it can only mean one thing—you're going downhill." She's tired, but she no longer wants to use that as an excuse for not putting in the work to make her life and her relationship a bigger priority. (Besides, who isn't tired these days?) She's realizing that being stagnant can feel more draining than coasting. She's scared to think about mixing up her routine—but she's scared not to. She's ready for the challenge.

BUILD YOUR MARRIAGE MUSCLE

Here's a scenario I see often with my clients: They spend years dreaming of goals and working hard to achieve them—but when they get close to making those dreams a reality, their fears and inhibitions spring up and blur their vision. Their gremlins try to convince them that they never really *wanted* what they feel they want and pursuing the goal is therefore a waste of their energy. Gremlins intrude, hold us back, and drain us; they deliver self-defeating messages like "Who are you to think you can do that?" or "You're going to fail if you try that."

I'm sure you've seen this pattern in another person (or perhaps have experienced it yourself): Someone has the opportunity to do something she has always talked about doing, and when the dream looks as if it may happen, she backs down or backs out.

Stepping into your goals and your greatness can feel terrifying because you are not only accountable to yourself and to the ideas that you have clung to (in some cases, for years), but you may feel that if you "fail," you will have nothing else to look forward to. Often when we move toward a goal like a new job or a change we want to make in our relationship, we feel uncomfortable or vulnerable. And this sense of discomfort is how we know that taking the risk is stretching us—and working. When you go the gym and exercise new muscles, you feel it the next day. Your body aches, and you may move more slowly and awkwardly when you wake up, but that's generally confirmation that you are building new muscles and getting stronger.

Like any good workout regimen, building your marriage muscle requires repetitions of effective routines and new exercises to stay in shape. Once you get used to the new exercises, you won't feel the burn like you used to. In fact, you will start to crave the challenge and miss it when you get off track. New routines that are at first daunting become priorities once we acclimate and see how they are serving us over the long run.

IMMEDIATE GRATIFICATION VERSUS LONG-TERM FULFILLMENT

Thousands of years ago Aristotle warned us not to confuse immediate gratification with long-term fulfillment and not to get sidetracked by external things—such as money, power, ego, fame, or status—that often distract us from living authentically and purposefully. Studies consistently show that these things do not give us intrinsic value or enduring happiness. This reminds me of humorist Art Buchwald's famous expression, "The best things in life are not things."

Without seeing the big picture of our relationship and investing in it, we lack the meaning and intention behind marriage and family. Without realizing our contribution as individuals, we will not feel a sense of purpose or passion in the world.

Once we choose a perspective of long-term fulfillment and move away from building a life based on immediate gratification (which powerfully colors our first love stage with our partners and all of the crushes we have on other men when we are married), and once we invest in our most important relationships with ourselves, our husband, our family, and our community, we are in balance.

With a long-term view of partnership, we are better able to weather small storms when we are not feeling in sync with our spouses. And let's face it, we will not always be on the same page . . . or chapter!

As Raquel reflects on her marriage today, she says she's gained more clarity on alternative ways to approach the points of contention with her husband and how to become more patient with herself. She is ready to set new expectations and make new commitments. She wants to take personal steps toward her passions that will make her more aligned with her wants. In doing so, she will invite more balance and joy into her home. She realizes now that her marital bliss starts with herself.

"For me, marriage used to represent all the things I didn't get to be when I was single," she observed. "Once I settled down, I gave myself permission not to engage in the world. I allowed myself to be lazy. I'm realizing now that that's not a good thing. I want to be comfortable in my marriage—but I'm sick of the blahs. I want to find my turn-on again. I owe that to my husband, my daughter, myself."

BALANCE

The other day I wondered how I got anything done before I had e-mail and my smart phone; then, a moment later, I wondered how I get anything done *with* those devices today. It's difficult to effectively manage and navigate our schedules and all of the factors competing for our attention and still make our relationships a priority. When we don't, however, our quality of life diminishes.

Of course, we can't expect our lives to resemble the way we lived before we added the roles of wife and/or mother to our daily routines. As with everything, we need to move away from an all-or-nothing mentality and remember that there is often a third (or fourth or fifth!) option that will help us produce better and more effective results. We are creatures of habit, after all, and need to be reminded to think and climb outside of our boxes.

In Chapter 3, I asked you to think of your life pie and consider how effectively you are balancing each of its slices. Now I want you to consider your marriage pie. The slices, of course, may also be sweet and sour. If you had to divide up this pie, the pieces might include Communication, Fun, Sex, Parenting, Family and Friends, Partnership, Housework, and Personal

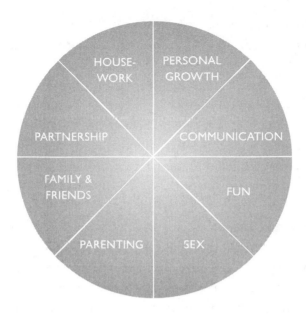

Growth. How do you rank each section of that pie? Where is there a lack of balance? Where do the numbers have to go up? What do you think will happen if they don't?

What steps can you take to increase each number in your marriage pie? As with any goal, you may have to say no to something (like working past 7:00 p.m.) in order to say yes to a better marriage.

THE REAL HOUSEWIVES OF AMERICA

I'm one of the worst housewives out there. I kill all plants, I can't decorate (when I lived alone I only hung stuff where there were already nails), and I get squeamish when I have to scrub a dirty pot. I hate routine and get anxious thinking about the suburbs. Some babies scare me. My favorite thing to make for dinner is a reservation.

My contribution as "wife" looks different from traditional definitions or even the definition I had before I got married. In my role, I try to be present for my husband and family. I think of his needs when I make decisions and his happiness when I make plans. He knows he can come to me with messy feelings, silly ideas, and crazy dreams and he won't be met with judgment. I see my role as one who offers support, guidance, comfort, and fun. I aim to embody and honor my contribution as partner and consider myself to be one of the CEOs of our family, but I know better than to run our partnership on my own. I want to keep learning, and I expect to be surprised. I want to represent home. I can't be that person, though, if my needs are hidden.

Many women feel guilty when they take care of their own needs. One woman I interviewed says she feels bad each time she gets a manicure without treating her 8-year old daughter to one, or when she leaves her kids at home with a babysitter. She loves being with her children and does not resent the sacrifices she makes on their behalf, but she continues to feel guilty when she focuses on her and her husband's needs.

Like worry, guilt is a response that requires energy and doesn't give any payoff. It festers and causes us to focus on, or obsess about, negative consequences. When guilt drives us to act in a way we don't really want to (or causes us to neglect something that we really want), the guilty feeling will likely be replaced with an even more unpleasant feeling—resentment.

When you feel guilty for doing something for yourself that you need—or even something that you *want* to do—take a moment to remember that you are responsible for your own happiness.

Don't wait for someone to give you what you need to give yourself.

Are you looking to be more connected to your husband? How can you get one step closer to your goal without relying on just your husband to fix it? Are you looking to be more engaged and excited about your life? How will you stay in touch with your own aspirations so that you are fulfilled and more connected to yourself? If it feels overwhelming to think about, consider that being authentic is perhaps the easiest thing you can be.

MARRIAGE MYTHS

One of the greatest myths of marriage is that as time goes on, the spark always dies. The other side of the spectrum is the idea that you must have problems if you're not feeling the electric love with your husband that used to consume you. Those theories didn't comfort me much before I decided to marry, and they don't serve any of us in long-term commitment.

Many of the myths floating around about what marriage *should* look like are getting us into trouble. If life is about expectations, these theories are not helping us:

Myth: Good marriages don't need work.

Truth: Good marriages value and commit to the work. Good marriages thrive on work.

Myth: After years with the same person, the spark always dies.

Truth: The spark flickers and sometimes reignites. Like anything in life, your marriage will ebb and flow.

Myth: Cross off everything on your to-do list before focusing on your marriage. Otherwise, you'll be too stressed to focus on it.

Truth: Your inbox will always be full, and you will never feel like you have the time to focus on your marriage. You have to make time.

Myth: The fantasy phase of your relationship has passed.

Truth: For those committed to their marriages, some of the best and most exciting chapters in marriage are yet to come.

There are so many theories on what marriage is or should be, even though the institution of marriage has changed substantially throughout the years and is framed differently across different cultures. Even in our own culture today, there are a number of variations on what is considered to be a desirable or normal marriage. Somehow, though, many of us cling to other peoples' definitions of marriage that may not resonate with or be relevant to us.

One popular theory about marriage is the idea that the union allows two halves to become whole and complete. And yet the couples I have interviewed who report being happiest in their relationships place great value on having an active life together *and* a dynamic life outside their partnerships. In their cases, their emphasis on being complete as individuals is incorporated into their definitions of what a happy and healthy marriage looks like.

Of course, there is no recipe for a perfect marriage, just as there is no formula for a perfect life. Let's move away from the idea of being perfect in any role and settle on a new word! I don't wish a perfect anything on anyone. Perfect is boring, inauthentic, and needy. Perfect is inaccessible and therefore leaves us frustrated, disconnected, or critical when we don't attain it. (Perfect isn't very fun, either.)

What three words come to mind when you think about your marriage? Are you happy with those words? What words do you want to represent the way you approach and conceive of your marriage?

The words I try to embody in my marriage include *connected, authentic,* and *fun.* Those words remind me of my deepest values and priorities. I don't always capture them, but I strive to be conscious of them so I can keep aligned with what is most important to me. My marriage is in beta, and I want to keep improving the model with better versions.

As you focus on the words that resonate most, consider this: How will you embody those qualities in your life and your marriage every day?

DATING EACH OTHER AGAIN

My 78-year-old Aunt Dorothy thinks it's essential to create room for romantic possibilities and future goals, no matter how old you are or how young your relationship is. She believes in dating her 83-year-old husband, Al.

Recently my aunt called my Uncle Al while she and I were driving home from dinner. I overheard her say, "Al, if you take a nice shower and wash your hair, I'll do the same thing . . . ." (I think this is geriatric code for *let's get it on*.)

I asked my aunt if this is a regular occurrence. "Mystery and intrigue need to be part of every marriage, Andrea," she responded, adding, "But I don't do this kind of thing all the time . . . . I wouldn't want Al to miss sleeping. I'd feel horrible!"

My aunt and uncle often call each other with a quick "Just want to let you know I'm thinking of you." They've been together for more than 40 years. If you overheard them, you might think they were just a few months into dating. This closeness doesn't happen by chance. My aunt told me that she creates the connection she craves.

CAPTURE YOUR CONNECTION

When I witness clients and friends experiencing the fantasy of new puppy love, I have to admit that I experience a twinge of longing. I miss the euphoric feeling of a powerful new attraction and the giddy sleep deprivation.

While it's not practical to stay in that heightened love-drug state, as we have discovered, occasionally reminding ourselves of the person we fell hard for is essential to keeping our connection intact. If we never invite nostalgia in, we get caught up in our daily routines and may forget why we decided to embark on the crazy journey of marriage with our partners.

One of my friends returned to the college town where she and her spouse fell in love and documented all of their old date spots in an album called "Us" that she updates frequently. She captured photos of the classroom where they originally met, the spot where they had their first kiss (which is now a coffeehouse, not a bar), and the theater where they used to (barely) watch movies on dates.

There are many pages and editions of this photo book, and my friend intends to fill it each year with more memories. She's aware that she is currently living in a cherished memory— something she will later reflect on and probably romanticize. She finds it exciting to see the number of blank pages that she and her partner will fill together.

Capturing memories is also important to my friend Esther and her family. Esther's husband is a stepdad to her first child, and he created a tradition in which he and his stepdaughter contribute to an album of experiences they have shared. Esther maintains that capturing positive memories helps her family stay close. The way that Esther and her family celebrate each other is embodied in one of Esther's favorite quotations, from Milan Kundera's *The Book of Laughter and Forgetting:* "For what is our identity? The sum total of everything we remember."

BUILD YOUR OWN HAPPILY EVER AFTER

When we are dating and falling in love with someone new, we get wrapped up in the fantasy and fairy tale of what may happen between us. We idealize the other person and perhaps our connection.

We know that the chemicals in our brain that are activated during love are the same ones that light up when we are addicted to a substance, and we know that under the influence of those chemicals, we don't think as clearly or as critically as usual. We recognize, intellectually, that this romantic—or more accurately ro-*manic*—stage of love isn't sustainable. And yet, some of us become disillusioned or confused years into our relationship when the horse gallops off into the sunset without us astride it and when our Prince Charming transforms into a mere mortal. With morning breath.

If you don't think you can afford the investment of time or energy that your marriage requires to continue to move forward, so that you are still excited to be with your spouse and inspired by the possibilities in your relationship, consider that you cannot afford *not* to. Intimacy and communication are cornerstones of any marriage. As they break down, relationships break up.

Relationships *are* work. But the work of taking risks together, of making discoveries about each other as a unit and as individuals, can be more than fulfilling—it can be thrilling. Once we commit to a long-term relationship, our connection with our partners becomes richer, more passionate, and more meaningful. It's powerful to co create a life with another person—and to help that person reach his or her potential.

Don't wait for disaster to strike before you recapture the dream that made you relinquish your single status. Don't settle just because you settled down. Build your own happily ever after.

ACKNOWLEDGMENTS

While working on this book, I loved reading the marriage studies, researching the science of love and reviewing the data; but it was the women I interviewed who taught me the most about modern marriage. They spoke with amazing candor and invited me into their homes to get a glimpse into their experiences as wives, mothers, and women. Each of them knows that marriage is a living institution, full of the proverbial ups and downs, and each is committed to creating the best marriage—and life—she aspires to have. There are too many women to mention here, but I thank them for contributing their insights to my book.

I thank my parents, Marilyn and Peter Syrtash, for teaching me so much about life, partnership, and family. I once heard that one of the most important things a child can witness is the love her parents have for each other. I feel blessed to have had marriage modeled so well.

My mother, the English teacher, has become my first stop for editing. She marked up the pages of my first school assignment, and I still count on her to catch my mistakes and compliment passages that she finds interesting. (She's incredibly biased and seems to find almost everything I write entertaining, but I don't mind.) I will be lucky if I become a mother as good as she was and is.

My dad, who wanted me to be a dentist like him (I had to remind him when I was 24 years old that I would have to go back to eighth grade to get some science requirements if I wanted to practice dentistry), has been incredibly supportive of my unusual career path. These days, he'll show you clips of me on TV every chance he gets. He teaches me so much about working hard and taking risks.

My sister, Veronica Syrtash, is a wonderful sister, writer, and editor. As my older sister, she offers perspective on my work that is tremendously helpful, and there are few things I want to do in life without her input. (I even Skype her to make sure my outfit matches.) She got married this year to a great guy named Jason, and I've enjoyed learning from them about how fun marriage can be. (They actually have dance parties for two in their living room!)

Speaking of exceptional editors, I must mention mine at Rodale—Julie Will. Julie is amazingly intelligent and has the ability to deepen and broaden my ideas, even when I'm sure I have nothing else to say. I don't know that she sleeps enough, but I appreciate that she's always made time to process ideas with me when I've wanted (and needed) her perspective. Anyone who knows her would agree—she's the best.

My agent, Ryan Fischer-Harbage, believed in me when I didn't even know if I needed an agent (ha!). He's an extraordinary agent, an amazing mentor, and a great friend. He teaches "selling your first book" seminars, and I'm always compelled to sign up. He's taught me so much.

I thank the fabulous team at Rodale, including Yelena Nesbitt, Aly Mostel, Kate Bellody, Marie Crousillat, Jessica Lee, Sasha Smith, Paula Brisco, Nancy N. Bailey, and Christina Gaugler, who consistently work hard to support my books' vision. They're smart and passionate, and they "get" me. I've always enjoyed Rodale's "live your whole life" message and am grateful to be aligned with such a quality publisher.

Thank you to Genevieve Lill, Melanie Gorman, and the rest of the fabulous YourTango.com team, who conducted some research on behalf of my book. YourTango.com is a great resource for relationships, and I love working with them. Thank you to Regina Miller, who launched a cool relationship platform called "Tokii," for sharing some of her site's research with me. I also thank the Coaches Training Institute and the Enneagram Institute for inspiring some of the exercises I used in *Cheat on Your Husband*.

I disappeared into my writing cave to work on this book, and my friends and family have been so patient and supportive. There are too many to mention, but I would like to highlight just a few friends who provided valuable feedback on my work: Steve MacKay, Jeff Wilser, Rebecca Raphael, Janna Harowitz— I'm so lucky to have you in my life.

To my Syrtash, Gaudin, and Mintz uncles, aunts, and cousins (and to my family in Budapest!): I'm sorry we don't live closer, but I love that when we're together, we fall back into place. To my in-laws, Ralph and Mimi Paoli, Tanya and Rob, Nola and Ness, David and Alex, and the extended Paoli-Harari family—one reason I love being married to Michael is that I get to have you in my life.

And finally, I must thank my husband, Michael. My previous book, *He's Just Not Your Type (And That's a Good Thing)* was inspired by him, and he inspires me every day. He challenges me, supports me, nurtures me, teases me, and always makes me feel beautiful (even when there's toilet paper stuck to the bottom of my shoe or peanut butter in my hair). Bo, you are certainly an acquired taste, and I'm hooked. I love you more every day.

ABOUT THE AUTHOR

Andrea Syrtash is an advice writer and relationship expert. She has contributed to more than a dozen relationship advice books, is the editor of *How to Survive the Real World* and *How to Survive Your In-Laws,* and the author of *He's Just Not Your Type (And That's a Good Thing).* Andrea has contributed to numerous popular sites including Oprah.com, Yahoo! and the Huffington Post, and she is the on-air host of *On Dating,* produced by NBC Digital Studios. She has shared relationship advice in various media outlets across the country including CBS's *The Early Show,* the *Today* show, VH1, TV Land, Martha Stewart Radio, and NPR. Her advice has also appeared in *Redbook, Marie Claire, People Style Watch, Women's Health, Cosmopolitan,* the *San Francisco Chronicle, USA Today,* the *Washington Post,* and the *Seattle Post Intelligencer.* Andrea is passionate about helping women live more authentically—in life and in love. She lives in Brooklyn, New York, with her husband. Visit Andrea at www.andreasyrtash.com.